Atlas of World History

The First Civilizations
to 500 BCE

BROWN
BEAR
BOOKS

Published by Brown Bear Books Limited

An imprint of:
The Brown Reference Group Ltd
68 Topstone Road
Redding
Connecticut 06896
USA
www.brownreference.com

© 2009 The Brown Reference Group Ltd

ISBN: 978-1-933834-65-8

Editorial Director: Lindsey Lowe
Senior Managing Editor: Tim Cooke
Managing Editor: Rachel Tisdale
Editor: Clare Colinson
Designer: Rob Norridge

Library of Congress Cataloging-in-Publication Data available upon request

Picture Credits

Cover Image
Shutterstock: Ian Stewart

Artwork © The Brown Reference Group Ltd

The Brown Reference Group Ltd has made every effort to trace copyright holders of the pictures used in this book. Anyone having claims to ownership not identified above is invited to contact The Brown Reference Group Ltd.

Printed in the United States of America

Contents

Introduction   4

The World in 2000 in BCE   6

The World in 1000 BCE   8

The World in 500 BCE   10

Peopling the Earth   12

The Rise of Agriculture   16

Farmers of the Middle East   20

Advanced Farmers of
    the Middle East   24

Cities of Mesopotamia   30

The First Empires   34

Hittites and Assyrians   38

Assyria and Babylon   44

The Bible Lands   50

Achemenid Persia   54

Ancient Egypt: Middle and
    New Kingdoms   58

Neolithic Europe   64

Bronze Age Europe   70

First Civilizations of
    the Mediterranean   76

Phoenicia and Greece   80

Greek City–States   84

Etruscans, Greeks,
    and Carthaginians   88

South Asia   92

East Asia   96

The Americas   100

Glossary   106

Further Research   108

Index   110

Introduction

Atlas of World History **forms part of the Curriculum Connections series. The six volumes of this set cover all the major periods of the World History curriculum: The First Civilizations (4,000,000–500 BCE); The Classical World (500 BCE–600 CE); The Middle Ages (600–1492); The Early Modern World (1492–1783); Industrialization and Empire (1783–1914); and World Wars and Globalization (1914–2010).**

About this set

Each volume in *Atlas of World History* features thematic world and regional maps. All of the regional maps are followed by an in-depth article.

The volume opens with a series of maps that provide an overview of the world at particular dates. They show at-a-glance how the shape of the world changed during the period covered in the book. The rest of the volume is divided into regional sections, each of which covers a continent or part of a continent. Within each section, maps appear in broadly chronological order. Each map highlights a particular period or topic, which the accompanying article explains in a concise but accurate summary.

Within each article, two key aids to learning are located in sidebars in the margins of each page:

Curriculum Context sidebars indicate that a subject has particular relevance to certain key state and national World and American history guidelines and curricula. They highlight essential information or suggest useful ways for students to consider a subject or to include it in their studies.

Glossary sidebars define key words within the text.

At the end of the book, a summary Glossary lists the key terms defined in the volume. There is also a list of further print and Web-based resources and a full volume index.

About this book

The First Civilizations is a fascinating guide to the history of humankind from the time of our earliest ancestors to the thriving civilizations of the fifth century BCE.

The volume begins with overview maps that chart the shifting pattern of human settlement and the rise and fall of states, also reviewing the role played by such innovations as agriculture, metallurgy, and literacy.

The regional maps that follow look more closely at the great events of the period: the emergence of the first cities in the Middle East, the biblical kingdoms, ancient Egypt, the Zhou civilization of China. There is also coverage of less familiar histories, such as those of Neolithic Europe, the Indus Valley civilizations, and the Chavín culture of Peru.

TYPOGRAPHICAL CONVENTIONS	
World maps	
FRANCE	state or empire
Belgian Congo	dependency or territory
Mongols	tribe, chiefdom or people
Anasazi culture	cultural group
Regional maps	
HUNGARY	state or empire
Bohemia	dependency or territory
Slavs	tribe, chiefdom or people
ANATOLIA	geographical region
⚔	battle
•	site or town

The World in 2000 BCE

By 2000 BCE farming was practiced on every continent and independent kinship-based farming societies were dominant in southeast Asia, north Africa, northern Europe, and parts of Mesoamerica. Large-scale hierarchical chiefdoms were established in the Middle East, southwest–central Europe, China, and the Andes. The first cities, states, and civilizations had emerged in Mesopotamia, Egypt, and the Indus valley.

Greenland

Arctic marine mammal hunters

Aleuts

Iceland

early Bronze Age
Unetice culture

Archaic Amerindian
hunter-gatherers

Bell Beaker culture
(late Neolithic fa

Berb

palace

Pasto

Hawaiian
Islands

Bahamas

Cuba
Jamaica
Hispaniola
Puerto Rico

maize farming replacing
hunting and gathering

tropical
hunter-g

Valdivia
tradition

Aspero
tradition

Archaic Amerindian
hunter-gatherers

Chinchoros
tradition

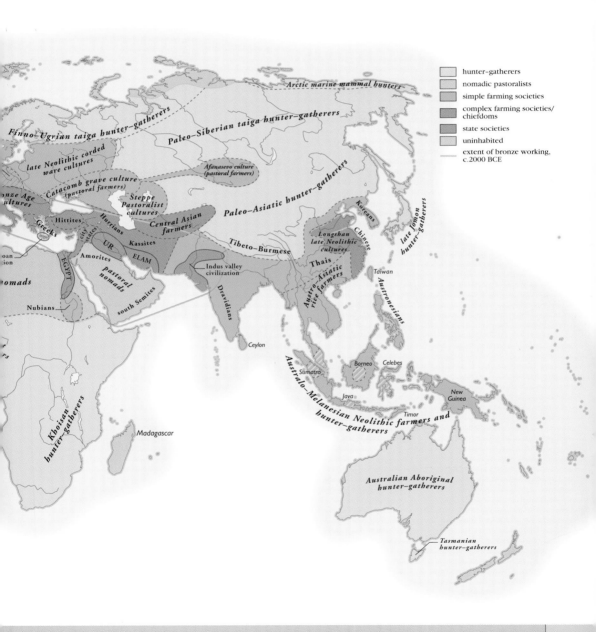

hunter-gatherers
nomadic pastoralists
simple farming societies
complex farming societies/
chiefdoms
state societies
uninhabited
extent of bronze working,
c.2000 BCE

Arctic marine mammal hunters

Finno–Ugrian taiga hunter–gatherers

Paleo–Siberian taiga hunter–gatherers

late Neolithic corded
ware cultures

Afanasevo culture
(pastoral farmers)

Catacomb grave culture
(pastoral farmers)

Paleo–Asiatic hunter–gatherers

Bronze Age
cultures

Steppe
Pastoralist
cultures

Central Asian
farmers

Koreans

late Jomon
hunter–gatherers

Hittites

Hurrians

Greeks

city
states

UR

Kassites

ELAM

Longshan
late Neolithic
cultures

Chinese

oan
tion

Amorites

pastoral
nomads

Indus valley
civilization

Tibeto–Burmese

Thais

Taiwan

omads

Egypt

Austro–
Asiatic
rice farmers

Austronesians

Nubians

south Semites

Dravidians

Ceylon

Borneo

Celebes

Sumatra

Java

New
Guinea

Khoisan
hunter–gatherers

Madagascar

Australo–Melanesian Neolithic farmers and
hunter–gatherers

Timor

Australian Aboriginal
hunter–gatherers

Tasmanian
hunter–gatherers

The World in 1000 BCE

By 1000 BCE migrations and invasions had caused widespread disruption in west Asia and Europe. While the ancient civilizations of the Middle East went into decline, the Phoenicians and Israelites became more powerful. Aryans had spread across northern India and the first great dynasty of China, the Shang, had been replaced by the Zhou. Meanwhile, the Olmec was the first civilization to appear in the Americas.

Greenland

Iceland

Arctic marine mammal hunters

Aleuts

sub-Arctic forest hunter–gatherers

Bron

west coast foraging hunting and fishing peoples

plateau fishers and hunter–gatherers

desert hunter–gatherers

plains bison hunters

Urnfield

Illy

T

Celtiberians

east woodlands hunter–gatherers

Poverty Point culture

Berbers

Hawaiian Islands

Pastoral ne

Bahamas

Olmec culture

Cuba
Jamaica

Hispaniola
Puerto Rico

maize farmers

Caribbean hunter–gatherers

cereal farme

Chorrera culture

manioc farmers (replacing hunter–gatherers)

Amazonian forest hunter–gatherers

El Paraiso culture

Chiripá culture

Chinchoros tradition

savanna hunter–gatherers

Andean hunter–gatherers

shellfish gatherers

pampas hunter–gatherers

shellfish gatherers and marine mammal hunters

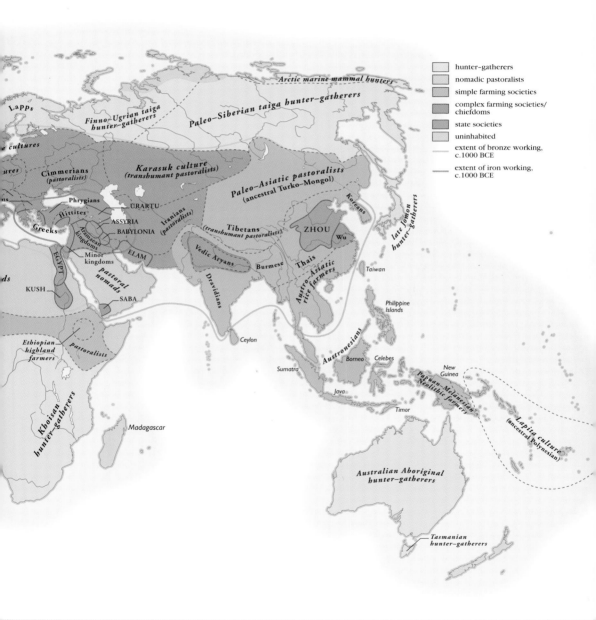

LaPPs

e cultures

ures

Cimmerians
(pastoralists)

Phrygians

Hittites

Greeks

URARTU

ASSYRIA

BABYLONIA

Aramaean
kingdoms

Minor
kingdoms

ELAM

EGYPT

KUSH

SABA

pastoral
nomads

Ethiopian
highland
farmers

pastoralists

ds

Khoisan
hunter-gatherers

Madagascar

Finno-Ugrian taiga
hunter-gatherers

Paleo-Siberian taiga hunter-gatherers

Arctic marine mammal hunters

Karasuk culture
(transhumant pastoralists)

Paleo-Asiatic pastoralists
(ancestral Turko-Mongol)

Iranians
(pastoralists)

Tibetans
(transhumant pastoralists)

Vedic Aryans

Dravidians

Burmese

Thais

Austro-Asiatic
rice farmers

ZHOU

Wu

Koreans

late Jomon
hunter-gatherers

Taiwan

Philippine
Islands

Austronesians

Borneo

Celebes

New
Guinea

Sumatra

Java

Timor

Papuan-Melanesian
Neolithic farmers

Lapita culture
(ancestral Polynesian)

Ceylon

Australian Aboriginal
hunter-gatherers

Tasmanian
hunter-gatherers

hunter-gatherers

nomadic pastoralists

simple farming societies

complex farming societies/
chiefdoms

state societies

uninhabited

extent of bronze working,
c.1000 BCE

extent of iron working,
c.1000 BCE

The World in 500 BCE

By 500 BCE west Asia was dominated by the Persians, whose empire extended from Egypt to the Indus. Meanwhile, the city–states of Greece had entered a period of intellectual creativity unparalleled in world history. The first states had appeared on the Ganges plain and China's Zhou dynasty had broken up into a number of warring states. In the Americas, the Maya and Zapotec cultures had emerged.

Greenland

Iceland

Arctic marine mammal hunters

sub-Arctic forest hunter-gatherers

Aleuts

west coast foraging, hunting and fishing peoples

Plateau fishers and hunter-gatherers

desert hunter-gatherers

plains bison hunters

east woodlands hunter-gatherers

Adena complex

Hawaiian Islands

maize farmers

Bahamas

Cuba

Jamaica

Hispaniola

Puerto Rico

Caribbean hunter-gatherers

Zapotec culture

Olmec culture

Maya

maize farmers

manioc farmers

Chorrera culture

Chavin culture

Paracas culture

Chinchoros tradition

Yaya–Mama religious tradition

savanna hunter-gatherers

shellfish gatherers

Andean hunter-gatherers

pampas hunter-gatherers

shellfish gatherers and marine mammal hunters

Hallstatt (Celt

Etruscans

Greeks

Celtiberians

Italics

CARTHAGINIAN

Berbers

Pastoral nom

cereal farmers

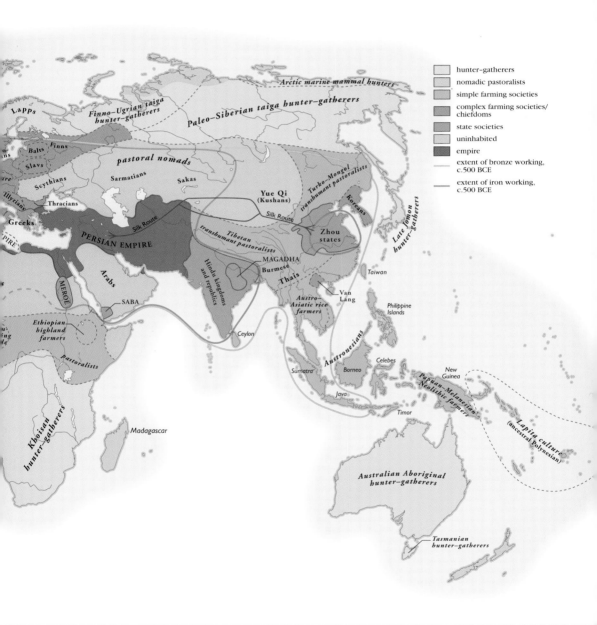

hunter-gatherers
nomadic pastoralists
simple farming societies
complex farming societies/chiefdoms
state societies
uninhabited
empire
extent of bronze working, c.500 BCE
extent of iron working, c.500 BCE

Arctic marine mammal hunters

Lapps

Finno–Ugrian taiga hunter-gatherers

Paleo-Siberian taiga hunter-gatherers

Balts
Finns
Slavs
Scythians
Illyrians
Thracians
Greeks

pastoral nomads

Sarmatians
Sakas

Turko-Mongol transhumant pastoralists

Yue Qi (Kushans)

Silk Route

Koreans

PERSIAN EMPIRE

Silk Route

transhumant pastoralists

Tibetan transhumant pastoralists

Zhou states

Late Jōmon hunter-gatherers

MEROË

Arabs

Hindu kingdoms and republics

MAGADHA

Burmese

Thais

SABA

Austro–Asiatic rice farmers

Van Lang

Taiwan

Philippine Islands

Ethiopian highland farmers

Ceylon

pastoralists

Austronesians

Celebes

New Guinea

Papuan–Melanesian Neolithic farmers

Sumatra
Borneo
Java
Timor

Lapita culture (ancestral Polynesian)

Khoisan hunter-gatherers

Madagascar

Australian Aboriginal hunter-gatherers

Tasmanian hunter-gatherers

Peopling the Earth

Anatomically modern humans (*homo sapiens*) had first appeared in Africa by 135,000 years ago (ya). By 10,000 years ago, humans inhabited most parts of the world.

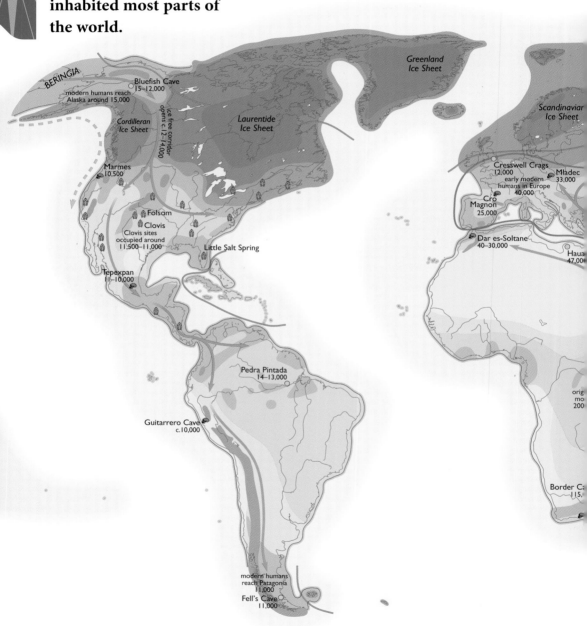

BERINGIA

Bluefish Cave
15–12,000

modern humans reach
Alaska around 15,000

Cordilleran
Ice Sheet

ice free corridor
opens c.12–14,000

Laurentide
Ice Sheet

Greenland
Ice Sheet

Scandinaviar
Ice Sheet

Cresswell Crags
12,000
early modern
humans in Europe
40,000

Mladec
33,000

Cro
Magnon
25,000

Dar es-Soltane
40–30,000

Haua
47,000

Marmes
10,500

Folsom

Clovis
Clovis sites
occupied around
11,500–11,000

Little Salt Spring

Tepexpan
11–10,000

orig
mo
200

Pedra Pintada
14–13,000

Guitarrero Cave
c.10,000

Border Ca
115,

modern humans
reach Patagonia
11,000

Fell's Cave
11,000

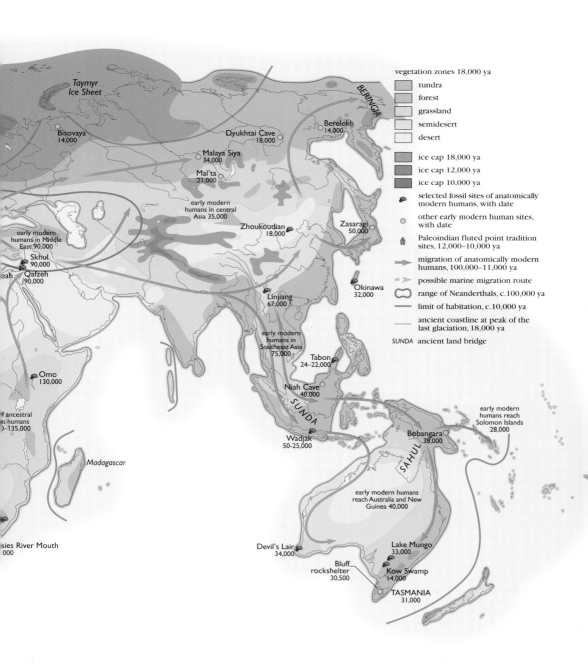

vegetation zones 18,000 ya

tundra
forest
grassland
semidesert
desert

ice cap 18,000 ya
ice cap 12,000 ya
ice cap 10,000 ya

selected fossil sites of anatomically modern humans, with date

other early modern human sites, with date

Paleoindian fluted point tradition sites, 12,000–10,000 ya

migration of anatomically modern humans, 100,000–11,000 ya

possible marine migration route

range of Neanderthals, c.100,000 ya

limit of habitation, c.10,000 ya

ancient coastline at peak of the last glaciation, 18,000 ya

SUNDA ancient land bridge

Taymyr Ice Sheet

BERINGIA

Bisovaya
14,000

Dyukhtai Cave
18,000

Berelekh
14,000

Malaya Siya
34,000

Mal'ta
21,000

early modern humans in central Asia 35,000

Zhoukoudian
18,000

Zasaragi
50,000

early modern humans in Middle East 90,000

Skhul
90,000

eah

Qafzeh
90,000

Omo
130,000

f ancestral n humans 0–135,000

Okinawa
32,000

Línjiang
67,000

early modern humans in Southeast Asia 75,000

Tabon
24–22,000

Niah Cave
40,000

SUNDA

Madagascar

Wadjak
50–25,000

Bobangara
38,000

SAHUL

early modern humans reach Solomon Islands 28,000

early modern humans reach Australia and New Guinea 40,000

sies River Mouth 000

Devil's Lair
34,000

Bluff rockshelter
30,500

Lake Mungo
33,000

Kow Swamp
14,000

TASMANIA
31,000

Peopling the Earth

Modern humans, *Homo sapiens sapiens*, first appeared in Africa between 200,000 and 135,000 years ago. By 90,000 years ago they lived in the Middle East; by 75,000 years ago they were in east Asia, and by 40,000 in Europe and Australasia. By the end of the Ice Age 10,000 years ago, only some oceanic islands, Antarctica, and some parts of the high Arctic remained uninhabited.

Two rival explanations have been offered for the origins of anatomically modern humans.

Parallel evolution

One explanation argues that the modern human races developed directly from the regional *Homo erectus* populations: modern Africans evolved from *Homo erectus* via African archaic *Homo sapiens*, modern Europeans from *Homo erectus* via European archaic *Homo sapiens* and Neanderthals, and so on. Critics point out that parallel evolution of this sort over such a wide area is implausible and that there is no supporting fossil evidence.

The "out of Africa" model

The second explanation, known as the single-origin or "out of Africa" model, is supported by genetic evidence suggesting that all modern humans derive from African ancestors who lived between about 285,000 and 150,000 years ago, and that all modern non-African humans are descendants of a single group of this ancestral population that migrated out of Africa around 100,000 years ago. According to this model, the descendants of this group spread across Eurasia.

Fossil and archeological evidence

The "out-of-Africa" model is more compatible with the fossil and archeological evidence than the parallel

Homo erectus

An extinct species of humans that lived from about 1.8 million years ago.

Neanderthal

An extinct humanlike species that lived between about 150,000 and 35,000 years ago.

Curriculum Context

Students learning about current and past theories regarding the emergence of modern humans might be asked to describe the "out of Africa" model.

evolution explanation. The earliest-known fossils of modern humans outside Africa date to about 90,000 years ago and were found in Israel. Only in Africa have forms intermediate between archaic and modern humans been found. In Europe, Neanderthals and early modern humans formed distinct populations that coexisted for over 10,000 years: the Neanderthals did not evolve into modern humans. In east and southeast Asia, the *Homo erectus* populations were replaced by modern humans with no trace of intermediate forms.

Curriculum Context

Fossil records are important evidence in the study of the evolution of humankind.

Moving east

When the first modern humans reached the Middle East, the global climate was beginning to enter one of the most severe glacial periods of the Ice Age. Human technology was probably inadequate for survival in the Arctic climates of Europe and central Asia, and these areas were left to the hardier Neanderthals. Instead the moderns moved east, reaching China and southeast Asia around 75,000 years ago. By 40,000 years ago they had reached New Guinea and Australia, probably by a series of island-hopping voyages.

From Europe and Asia to the Americas

About 40,000 years ago, modern humans moved into Europe. By this time they had evolved modern mental characteristics and sufficient technology to flourish on the frigid Eurasian steppes and tundras. By 35,000 years ago hunting bands had reached deep into central Asia and by 20,000 years ago others, perhaps moving north from China, had entered northeastern Siberia. The area now covered by the Bering Straits was a cold plain which some bands crossed to reach the Americas by 15,000 years ago. Between 14,000 and 12,000 years ago hunting–gathering bands— the Paleoindians—could reach the heart of North America. The Paleoindians spread rapidly through the Americas and had reached Patagonia in South America by 11,000 years ago.

Curriculum Context

The migration of early humans from Asia to the Americas is important in understanding how human communities populated the major regions of the world.

The Rise of Agriculture

For most of their early
history, humans were
hunter–gatherers.
Agriculture arose in many
parts of the world between
10,000 and 5000 BCE.

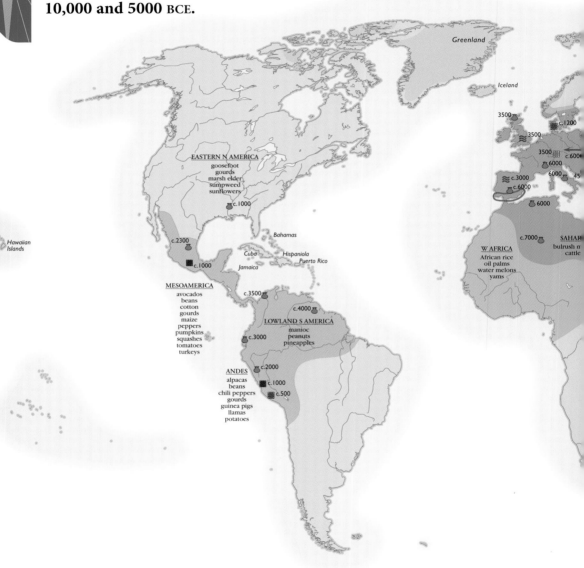

Greenland

Iceland

3500

c.1200

3500

3500

c.600

6000

6000

45

c.3000

c.6000

6000

EASTERN N AMERICA
goosefoot
gourds
marsh elder
sumpweed
sunflowers

c.1000

c.7000

SAHAR
bulrush m
cattle

Hawaiian
Islands

c.2300

Bahamas

W AFRICA
African rice
oil palms
water melons
yams

Cuba

Hispaniola

Puerto Rico

c.1000

Jamaica

MESOAMERICA
avocados
beans
cotton
gourds
maize
peppers
pumpkins
squashes
tomatoes
turkeys

c.3500

c.4000

LOWLAND S AMERICA
manioc
peanuts
pineapples

c.3000

ANDES
alpacas
beans
chili peppers
gourds
guinea pigs
llamas
potatoes

c.2000

c.1000

c.500

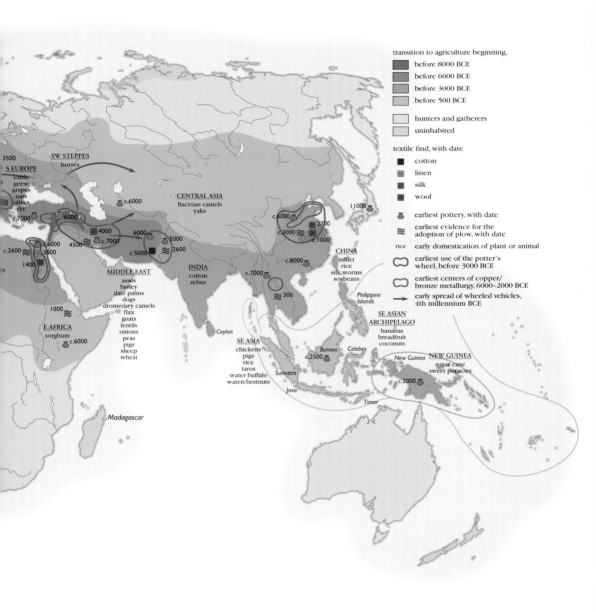

transition to agriculture beginning,

- before 8000 BCE
- before 6000 BCE
- before 3000 BCE
- before 500 BCE

- hunters and gatherers
- uninhabited

textile find, with date

- cotton
- linen
- silk
- wool

earliest pottery, with date

earliest evidence for the adoption of plow, with date

rice   early domestication of plant or animal

earliest use of the potter's wheel, before 3000 BCE

earliest centers of copper/ bronze metallurgy, 6000–2000 BCE

early spread of wheeled vehicles, 4th millennium BCE

3500

S EUROPE
cattle
geese
grapes
oats
olives
rye

c.7000

c.6000

c.2600

1400

E AFRICA
sorghum
c.6000

1000

SW STEPPES
horses

6500

4000

4500

c.7000

3500

c.6000

MIDDLE EAST
asses
barley
date palms
dogs
dromedary camels
flax
goats
lentils
onions
peas
pigs
sheep
wheat

c.6000

6000

c.5000

5000

2600

CENTRAL ASIA
Bactrian camels
yaks

INDIA
cotton
zebus

c.7000

300

Ceylon

SE ASIA
chickens
pigs
rice
taros
water buffalo
waterchestnuts

Sumatra

Java

c.6000

c.3000

c.8000

CHINA
millet
rice
silk worms
soybeans

2700

c.1000

11000

Philippine Islands

SE ASIAN ARCHIPELAGO
bananas
breadfruit
coconuts

Borneo
c.2500

Celebes

New Guinea
NEW GUINEA
sugar cane
sweet potatoes

c.2000

Timor

Madagascar

The Rise of Agriculture

Farming communities arose independently in many parts of the world as a response to environmental changes that followed the end of the Ice Age in about 10,000 BCE. The warmer climate was not an unmixed blessing: sea levels rose as the ice sheets melted, flooding huge areas of lowland hunting grounds. The savannas, steppes, and tundras, all abundant in big game, shrank as the forests advanced.

Hunter–gatherers
People who obtain most of their food by hunting wild animals and eating plants, nuts, and berries gathered from the wild.

In many areas, hunter–gatherers began to exploit small game birds, fish, and plants to a greater extent than before. It was among these communities that agriculture first arose.

Domestication of plants and animals
The first stage was probably planting the seeds of favored wild plant foods to guarantee their continuing availability. Next was the domestication of food plants by breeding strains with desirable characteristics. Because their seeds had a high carbohydrate content and were easy to store, the most important domesticated plant foods were strains of the cereals: wheat, barley, oats, rice, millet, and maize. Animal domestication began with the management and selective culling of wild herds. Penning the animals followed, then selective breeding.

Development of farming economies
Some communities of hunter–gatherers moved from casual cultivation of wild plants (incipient agriculture) to a full farming economy far more quickly than others. Farmers have to work harder than hunter–gatherers, and few made the transition willingly. Rising populations probably forced many to adopt cultivation to supplement wild food supplies. In the Fertile Crescent of the Middle East, where farming first developed, the transition from incipient agriculture

Fertile Crescent
The region extending from the foothills of Iraq's Zagros mountains through south Turkey, to western Syria, Lebanon, and Israel.

to dependence on domesticated cereals took only three centuries, 8000–7700 BCE, and domesticated animals replaced hunted wild animals a millennium later. In Mesoamerica a full farming way of life developed within a few centuries of the domestication of maize. In eastern North America hunting and gathering remained the main source of food for some three millennia after the first cultivation of domesticated food around 2500 BCE.

Social implications

The adoption of agriculture had far-reaching social implications. Farming peoples accumulated material possessions on a scale far beyond anything possible among most hunter–gatherers. As a result, differences in social status became more marked and the egalitarianism of hunter–gatherer society gave way to complex and hierarchical social structures. Most significantly, farming made possible an enormous increase in the human population. While the typical unit of hunter–gatherer society was the nomadic band of 30 to 50, simple farming methods could support villages of hundreds of people and intensive methods involving plowing and irrigation, towns of thousands.

Curriculum Context

The domestication of maize is important in understanding the development of complex farming societies in Mesoamerica.

Curriculum Context

A comparison of the social organization of hunter–gatherer and agrarian communities will help students gain a deeper understanding of early agricultural societies.

Technological developments

New tools, such as polished stone axes for clearing forest, hoes, sickles, and grindstones, appeared in early farming cultures. Pottery became common in early farming settlements where it was needed for storage and cooking. Pottery led to other technological breakthroughs: the kilns that were developed in some areas for baking pots also provided the means for smelting and casting metals—copper and gold first, then bronze, and finally iron. The wheel, too, was first used as an aid to making pottery; only later was it applied to transportation. The spinning and weaving of plant and animal fibers to make textiles also became important in early farming communities.

Farmers of the Middle East

Settlements of the Fertile Crescent were the first to cultivate cereals and by 7500 BCE communities with a full farming economy had developed.

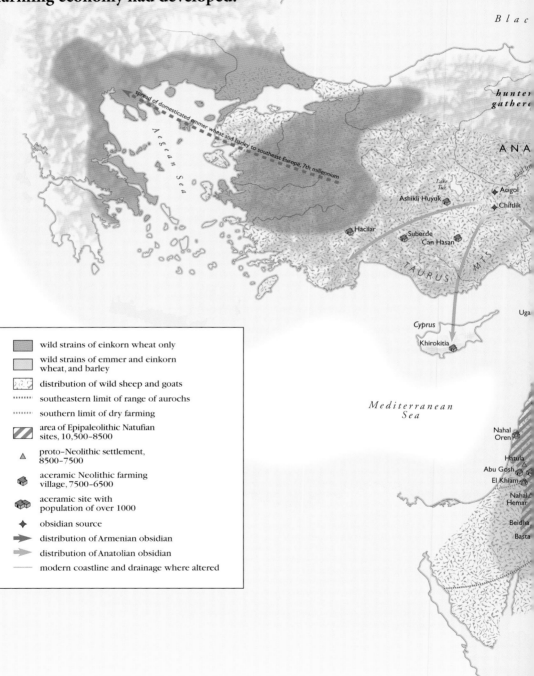

B l a c [k]

hunter gatherers

ANA[TOLIA]

spread of domesticated emmer wheat and barley to southeast Europe, 7th millennium

Aegean Sea

Kizil Irm[ak]

Lake Tuz

Ashikli Huyuk

◆ Acigol

◆ Chiftlik

Hacilar

Suberde
Can Hasan

T A U R U S   M T S

Uga[rit]

Cyprus

Khirokitia

M e d i t e r r a n e a n
S e a

Nahal Oren

Hatula

Abu Gosh

El Khiam

Nahal Hemar

Beidha

Basta

Legend

▨	wild strains of einkorn wheat only
▢	wild strains of emmer and einkorn wheat, and barley
▨	distribution of wild sheep and goats
....	southeastern limit of range of aurochs
....	southern limit of dry farming
▨	area of Epipaleolithic Natufian sites, 10,500–8500
△	proto–Neolithic settlement, 8500–7500
◈	aceramic Neolithic farming village, 7500–6500
◈◈	aceramic site with population of over 1000
✦	obsidian source
➤	distribution of Armenian obsidian
➤	distribution of Anatolian obsidian
——	modern coastline and drainage where altered

Sea

CAUCASUS MOUNTAINS

Kura

Caspian Sea

Araks

OLIA

Murat

Bingol

Nemrut Dag

Lake Van

Lake Urmia

Cafer Huyuk

Chayonu

Colux

Gritille

ZAGROS MOUNTAINS

Zawi Chemi Shanidar

Tell Aswad

Qermez Dere

Tigris

Great Zab

MESOPOTAMIA

Karim Shahir

Jarmo

Tell Mureybet

Abu Hureyra

Orontes

Euphrates

Bouqras

Ganj Dareh

Diyala

Tepe Abdul Hosein

Tepe Guran

Syrian Desert

Tamarkhan

Karkheh

Labwe

Tell Ramad

aisamoun

Ali Kosh

Choga Bonut

unhatta

Ain Ghazal

ericho

Persian Gulf

Farmers of the Middle East

The earliest communities to rely on farming for most of their food grew up in the area known as the Fertile Crescent in the Middle East. This is a region with good soils and light but reliable rainfall. Around 10,000 BCE the supply of cereals and nuts in the region was so rich that some hunter–gatherer populations could settle in semi-permanent villages.

Levant

The part of the Fertile Crescent that borders the Mediterranean Sea.

Curriculum Context

The need for increased yields to sustain the food supply is important in understanding the development of early agrarian communities.

First farmers

Among the sedentary hunter–gatherers of the Fertile Crescent region were the Natufians of the Levant, whose way of life developed about 10,500 BCE. Except for short stays at seasonal camps, the Natufians lived in villages of wooden huts with stone foundations. They hunted gazelle intensively but their staple food was wild cereals.

During the ninth millennium BCE the Natufians began to cultivate wild cereals close to their settlements. In some places, wild cereals may even have been introduced to areas where they did not naturally occur. The climate was changing and the natural range of wild cereals was shrinking, so these developments were probably an attempt to secure the food supply. Around 8000 BCE these early farmers learned to breed wild cereals selectively for characteristics that increased the yield. Within a few centuries domesticated strains of barley, emmer, and einkorn wheat had appeared.

The development of farming economies

As the population of these transitional, or "proto-Neolithic," farmers began to outstrip the environment's capacity to support the old lifestyle, the dependence on farming increased. By about 7500 BCE communities with a full farming economy had developed, marking the proper beginning of the Neolithic period or "New Stone Age."

Farming also began to develop in southern Anatolia and the Zagros mountains. In the mountains, hunter–gatherers intensified their management of flocks of wild sheep and goats. By the seventh millennium BCE, domesticated sheep and goats were an important part of the economy of villages such as Chayonu (now in eastern Turkey).

Further developments

Pottery appeared by 7000 BCE and its use had become widespread within five centuries. By this time bread wheat had also been developed, flax—the raw material of linen cloth—had been domesticated, as had the pig, and cattle were introduced from southeastern Europe, where farming was beginning.

Long-distance trade

The sedentary way of life meant that communities became less self-sufficient and long-distance trade, particularly in salt and toolmaking stone, became more important. The finest toolmaking stone, obsidian (volcanic glass), was traded over long distances. Obsidian from Anatolia has been found in early Neolithic sites almost as far south as the Red Sea, while obsidian from Lake Van reached the Mediterranean.

Jericho

One of the most impressive proto-Neolithic sites is at Jericho, now in modern Israel, where a walled settlement of 1,500 people had grown up near a permanent spring by about 8000 BCE. Domesticated barley and emmer wheat, pulses, and figs were cultivated, but wild animals were also important food sources. The people lived in huts built of sun-dried mud bricks, the earliest known use of what became the most important building material of the Middle East. Mud brick was easy to produce; when a house fell into disrepair it was simply knocked down and replaced by a new one. Over the centuries, successive rebuildings on the same site produced a high mound of debris, called a *tell* in Arabic, *huyuk* in Turkish, and *tepe* in Persian. These settlement mounds are the most characteristic archeological sites of the region.

Advanced Farmers of the Middle East

The expansion of farming settlements across the Mesopotamian plain after 6500 BCE is reflected in a series of cultures, each identified by a distinctive pottery style.

Black Sea

Karaoglan

ANATOLIA

Kızıl Irmak

Hagia Gala

Lake Tuz

Beycesultan

Arsla

Hacilar

Chatal Huyuk

Coyhan

Sakchago

Suberde

Can Hasan

Tarsus

Carchem

MTS

Mersin

Tell Judeideh

TAURUS

Abu

Rhodes

Ugarit

Orontes

Hama

Philia

Tell Sukas

LEVANT

Khirokitia

Tabbat al-Hammam

Cyprus

Arjoune

Byblos

Labwe

Mediterranean Sea

Tell Ramad

Kabri

Munhatta

Jericho

Ghrubba

Ghassul

Ashkelon

	earliest centers of copper working, 6000	≈	evidence of irrigation, c.6000
	spread of copper working by 4500	**Uruk**	Ubaid period temple
⌢	Hassuna culture, 6500–6000		early pottery kilns
⌢	Samarran culture, 6000–5500		find of Ubaid pottery outside main cultural area
⌢	Halafian culture, 6000–5400	✦	obsidian source
⌢	Ubaid culture, 5900–4300	✧	copper source
		⋯⋯	southern limit of dry farming
	settlement, though not necessarily occupied continuously throughout the period	—	modern coastline and drainage where altered
⬚	established before 6000		
⬚	established 6000–5400		
⬚	established 5400–4300		

C A U C A S U S   M O U N T A I N S

Kura

Murat

Araks

Tepecik
Norshuntepe
Tiki Tepe
Lake Van
Yanik Tepe
Lake Urmia
Tepe Seavan
Tell Turlu
Chagar Bazar
Tell Abu Dhahir
Yarim Tepe
Tepe Gawra
Hajii Firuz
Hasanlu
Tell Halaf
Kul Tepe
Nineveh
Banahilk
Tigris
Great Zab
Tell Hamman al-Turkman
Tell Azzo
Arpachiyeh
Shusharra
eyra
Tell Zaidan
Hassuna
Jarmo
MESOPOTAMIA
Euphrates
Tell Umm Dabaghiyeh
Diyala
Choga Maran
GodinTepe
Tepe Sialk
Bouqras
Tell Madhhur
Tepe Sarab
Tepe Giyan
Baghouz
Samarra
Tell Abadeh
Tepe Guran
Tell al-Sawwan
Choga Mami
Syrian Desert
Karkheh
Z A G R O S   M O U N T A I N S
Ali Kosh
Boneh Fazili
Choga Mish
Tell Uqair
Susa
Nippur
Lagash
Uruk
Tell Awayli
Hajji Muhammed
Ur
Tell al-Ubaid
Eridu

Persian Gulf

Advanced Farmers of the Middle East

By the time pottery came into widespread use in the Fertile Crescent, around 6500 BCE, the densest concentration of farming settlements was still to be found in the uplands of the Levant, the Zagros mountains, and southern Anatolia, where there was reliable rainfall. Most villages had only a few hundred inhabitants, relatively egalitarian social structures, and simple subsistence economies.

Curriculum Context

The characteristics of large settlements such as Chatal Huyuk are key to understanding how agricultural societies developed around the world.

Mesopotamia

"The Land Between the Rivers" lay between the Tigris and Euphrates rivers, in part of what is now Iraq. The area was home to several early civilizations.

Chatal Huyuk

An important exception was the town-sized settlement which grew up around 6700 BCE at Chatal Huyuk in modern Turkey. This settlement of densely packed mud-brick houses is the largest Neolithic settlement yet found. Long-distance trade in obsidian from nearby volcanoes, and improved agricultural yields resulting from the adoption of simple irrigation techniques, may have played a role in the town's growth. Chatal Huyuk had rich artistic traditions of wall-painting and sculpture, and a great many elaborately decorated shrines have been found. Many other crafts were practiced, including weaving, basketry, copper working (the earliest-known evidence of copper smelting has been found here), fine stone toolmaking, and pottery. Chatal Huyuk, however, was an unusual development. The local environment could not sustain long-term urban growth: the site was abandoned after about a thousand years and the pattern of dispersed settlements, typical of the rest of Neolithic Anatolia, was resumed.

The Hassuna culture

The conditions for sustainable urban growth were first achieved in Mesopotamia. Farming was still confined to the fringes of the Mesopotamian plain in 6500 BCE, but it had spread throughout the region by 5500 BCE. The expansion of farming settlements across the plain

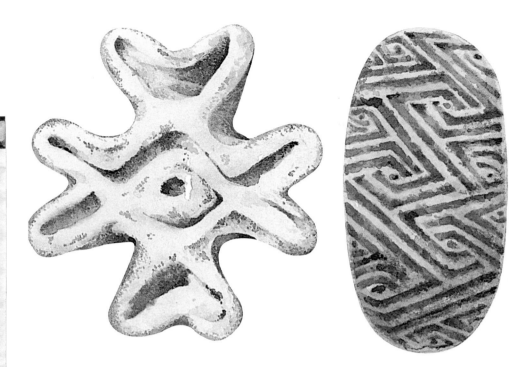

is reflected by a series of cultures. The first of these was the Hassuna culture (6500–6000 BCE), centered on northern Mesopotamia. The Hassuna people grew emmer, einkorn, and barley, and bred sheep, goats, and pigs. There is evidence for copper and lead smelting and the Hassuna culture was the earliest to produce painted pottery and fire it in purpose-built kilns. Stamp seals, later used widely in Mesopotamia to indicate ownership, were also first used in the Hassuna culture.

Clay stamps with incised decoration were found in Chatal Huyuk in Anatolia. They were probably used to print textiles.

The Halafian and Samarran cultures

The Hassuna culture was replaced around 6000 BCE by the Halafian culture. A storehouse excavated at Arpachiyeh, containing a concentration of fine pottery, jewelry, sculpture, and flint and obsidian tools, suggests that the Halafians were ruled by chiefs who amassed considerable personal wealth and controlled the community's trade contacts.

Curriculum Context

Students may be required to describe archeological evidence for the emergence of social class divisions in agricultural settlements in southwest Asia.

The influence of the Halafian culture was confined almost entirely to the dry farming zone but the same was not true of the contemporary, and overlapping, Samarran culture which developed around 6000 BCE to the south of the Hassunan area. The most significant achievement of this culture was the development of large-scale irrigation techniques such as canal-building. This boosted yields within the dry farming zone but, more importantly, allowed Samarran farmers to settle on the arid plains of central Mesopotamia.

The Ubaid culture

The earliest-known culture of the floodplain of the Tigris and Euphrates rivers in southern Mesopotamia, the Ubaid, developed around 5900 BCE and in its early stages showed clear affinities with the Samarran culture to the north. The Ubaid culture lasted over 15 centuries and laid the foundations of the later Sumerian civilization of southern Mesopotamia. The first inhabitants of this almost rainless region depended mainly on fishing, hunting, and herding, but the introduction of irrigation techniques from the north transformed the settlement pattern. Irrigation allowed the productive potential of southern Mesopotamia's fertile alluvial soils to be realized.

Plow technology

Productivity received another boost in the fifth millennium BCE with the invention of the plow. Intensive agriculture meant that the population rose rapidly and many new farming villages were founded. Some of these, like Eridu, the best known Ubaid site, had grown into small towns by the fifth millennium BCE.

Religious center

A simple shrine established at Eridu in early Ubaid times already displayed the distinctive features of later Mesopotamian temples: an ornamental facade, an offering table, and an altar for the statue of the god. The temple was rebuilt several times and by the end of the Ubaid period it had become a multi-roomed complex built on top of a 3.5-foot (1 m) high platform. Eridu functioned as a religious center for a number of surrounding hamlets, which it may have controlled through the spiritual power of a priesthood or by control of irrigation or trade.

Trade links

Southern Mesopotamia lacks many essential raw materials, including building timber, metals and stone for toolmaking (and, later for building and sculpture), and semiprecious stone: as a result trade links were of vital importance to—and helped to spread the influence of—the Ubaid culture. By 5400 BCE the Ubaid culture had replaced the Halafian culture in northern Mesopotamia, while Ubaid pottery manufactured around Ur has been found throughout the Persian Gulf region.

Accounting and writing

An important innovation of the Ubaid culture was to introduce an accounting system, based on clay tokens, a precursor of the first writing system. Although some form of social organization was needed for irrigation works and temple building, burial practices of the Ubaid period suggest that society was still basically egalitarian.

End of the Ubaid period

When the Ubaid period came to a close in about 4300 BCE, the population of southern Mesopotamia was still on the increase. The succeeding Uruk period saw the development of a far more complex and hierarchical society.

Cities of Mesopotamia

Mesopotamia became a center
of urbanization and cultural
innovation in the Uruk period,
with the first cities and city–
states emerging in Sumeria.

copper

*copper
from Anatolia*

Murat

Hassek Huyuk

Ceyhan

TAURUS MTS *silver*

Tell B

timber

Habuba Kabira

Orontes

Ebla

copper

Ugarit

shells

Cyprus

Hama

Euphrates

Syrian   Desert   **Mari**

Byblos

timber

Mediterranean Sea

KINGDOM
OF EGYPT
(c. 3000 BC)

*alabaster
diorite
gold*

Memphis

copper

▨ area of strongest Sumerian cultural influence	⊿ inscribed clay tablets (proto-Elamite script), 3100–2900	
⬭ kingdom of Lugalzagesi, c.2350	—— trade route	
🏛 city named in the Sumerian King List (compiled c.2100)	*copper* imports to Mesopotamia	
🏛 other city	grain exports from Mesopotamia	
Mari site of major temple	▨ area of alluvial soils	
<u>Kish</u> site of palace	—— modern coastline and drainage where altered	

origins of writing

⊳ hollow clay spheres and impressed
tablets (token system)

⊲ inscribed clay tablets (Sumerian
pictographic script), 3400–2900

obsidian

Caspian Sea

Lake
Van

*copper
tin
turquoise*

Hasanlu

*silver
tin*

Lake
Urmia

Great Zab

Tepe Gawra

Nineveh

Z A G R O S

Ashur

Nuzi

Hamazi

M
E
S
O
P
O
T
A
M
I
A

Tigris

Diyala

Gutians

Godin Tepe

Tepe Sialk

M O U N T A I N S

*carnelian
lapis lazuli
from Afghanistan*

Tell Gubba

Kassites

E L A M

Karkheh

textiles

Eshnunna

bitumen

Hit

Tutub
(Khafaje)

Tell Agrab

Der

Sippar

Akshak

Awan

Tell Uqair

Jemdet Nasr

Susa

Choga Mish

Kish

A K K A D

Abu Salabikh

S U M E R

Nippur

Adab

*grain
textiles*

Shuruppak

Umma

Girsu

Bad-tibira

Lagash

grain

Uruk

Larsa

Nina

Tell al-Ubaid

Anshan

Ur

Eridu

*chlorite
from Tepe Yahya
(southern Iran)*

Persian Gulf

*pearls
shells*

*carnelian
ivory
steatite
timber
from Meluhha
(Indus valley)*

Dilmun

Cities of Mesopotamia

The world's first cities and states emerged in the region of Sumeria in southern Mesopotamia in the Uruk period (4300–3100 BCE), named for the oldest and largest Sumerian city. States, with their social classes, centralized government, and well-organized trade, became important mechanisms for coordinating flood control (important in this region) and other public works.

Curriculum Context

Students learning about early civilizations may be asked to focus on the relationship between religion and the social and political order in Mesopotamia.

Curriculum Context

The development of occupational specializations in Sumerian cities is key to understanding the development of early civilizations.

Early Sumerian cities

Early Sumerian cities were dominated by temple complexes, and the priesthood probably took the lead in their organization. The Tigris and Euphrates rivers are subject to violent floods and unpredictable changes of course, events which must have seemed like the acts of capricious gods. The priests claimed to be able to propitiate the gods, and this may have given them the authority to be accepted as rulers of their cities.

Most Sumerian cities of the Uruk period had a population between two and eight thousand people, although Uruk itself, the largest, had over 10,000; by 2700 BCE this had risen to about 50,000. The food surpluses the farmers produced were great, and Sumerian society became the first to have the resources to support large numbers of people in specialist occupations: sculptors, potters, bronze-casters, stonemasons, bakers, brewers, and weavers.

The temples became centers of redistribution where the surplus food of the countryside and craft products were gathered to be given out as rations or traded abroad for raw materials that could not be found locally. These trade links ranged from India and Afghanistan to Egypt, and played an important part in spreading the influence of Sumerian civilization throughout the Middle East. It was a complex task to manage the redistribution of produce. Keeping track of all the transactions was beyond the ability of unaided memory and by around 3400 BCE a system of pictographic writing, probably derived from an earlier token system, had been developed.

The Early Dynastic period

Sumerian civilization entered a new and troubled phase in the Early Dynastic period (2900–2334 BCE). Massive defensive walls were built around the cities, bronze weapons were produced in increasing quantities, and war began to feature as a subject of official art. This period also saw writing applied to purposes other than administration, as rulers recorded their glorious deeds to ensure their posthumous reputations. The gap between rich and poor widened and slavery appears in the records for the first time. Secular leaders now appear alongside the priest-kings. These secular rulers built palaces next to the temple precincts, where they lived in opulence. In death they were given rich burials. Lacking the spiritual authority of the priesthood, the new secular rulers established their authority through law codes.

Rivalry between city–states

The martial spirit of Early Dynastic Sumeria was mainly a result of competition between city–states as the population density on the plains rose to saturation point. The early Early Dynastic period was dominated by rivalry between Kish, Uruk, and Ur. By 2500 BCE Mesilim of Kish was the nominal overlord of Sumeria. The dominance of Kish was ended around 2400 BCE by Eannatum of Lagash. A dispute between Lagash and Umma was resolved when Lagash was conquered by Lugalzagesi of Umma, who went on to carve out a kingdom in Sumeria and Akkad to the north. His kingdom lasted only about 16 years, but it effectively ended the period of independent city–states.

The First Empires

In the third millennium BCE
Sargon of Akkad was the
first king to unite people
of many different ethnic
and cultural identities to
create an entirely new kind
of state: an empire.

Hittites

Hattusas
(Boghazkoy)

Lake
Tuz

Puruskhanda

Kultepe
(Kanesh)

SUB.
Chaga
(Ashn

Harran

TAURUS MTS

Carchemish

Aleppo

Tuttul

Orontes

Ebla

Ugarit

Cyprus

LEVANT

Qatna

Syrian   Desert

Byblos

Tadmor
(Palmyra)

Mediterranean
Sea

Damascus

Megiddo

Lachish

EGYPT

Heliopolis

Memphis

Nile

	empire of Sargon "the Great" of Agade, c.2279
	territories possibly part of Sargon's empire
	empire of the Third Dynasty of Ur, 2112–2004
	Babylonian empire under Hammurabi, c.1750
	kingdom of Shamshi–Adad, c.1813–1781
	limit of Egyptian influence, c.1850
■	city

Kish   royal palace

▷   preserved palace archive of clay tablets

Ur   capital of empire

ziggurat

◆   Ur III, 2112–2004

◆   old Babylonian, 1900–1700

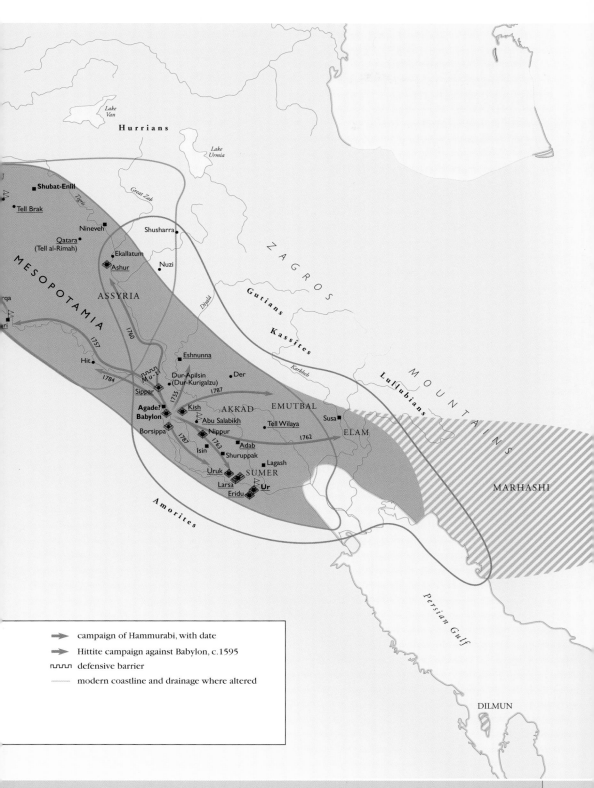

Lake Van

H u r r i a n s

Lake Urmia

Shubat-Enlil

• Tell Brak

Great Zab

Tigris

Nineveh

Shusharra

Qatara
(Tell al-Rimah)

• Ekallatum

M E S O P O T A M I A

Ashur

Nuzi

1760

A S S Y R I A

Diyala

G u t i a n s

Z A G R O S

1757

K a s s i t e s

qa

1784

Hit •

Eshnunna

Dur-Apilsin
(Dur-Kurigalzu)

Der

Karkheh

L u l l u b i a n s

Mari

Mu-t

Sippar

1755

1787

E M U T B A L

M O U N T A I N S

Agade? ■
Babylon

Kish

A K K A D

Susa

Borsippa

Abu Salabikh

Tell Wilaya

E L A M

1787

Nippur

1762

1763

Adab

Isin

Shuruppak

Lagash

M A R H A S H I

Uruk

S U M E R

Larsa

Eridu

Ur

A m o r i t e s

Persian Gulf

	campaign of Hammurabi, with date
	Hittite campaign against Babylon, c.1595
⌐⌐⌐	defensive barrier
——	modern coastline and drainage where altered

DILMUN

The First Empires

By the end of the Early Dynastic period Sumeria, though still wealthy and populous, was being overtaken by Akkad as the leading center of Mesopotamian civilization. The rise of Akkad is reflected in the career of the first great conqueror known to history, Sargon "the Great" of Agade, who reigned for 55 years, from 2334 to 2279 BCE.

Building an empire

How Sargon came to power is unknown but he may have staged a coup against his employer, the king of Kish. Having eliminated the most powerful ruler in Mesopotamia, Lugalzagesi of Umma and Uruk, Sargon went on to conquer the rest of Sumeria, Akkad, and Elam before pushing west to the Mediterranean and Anatolia. His empire reached its peak under his grandson Naram-Sin (r.2254–2218 BCE) but collapsed about 2193 BCE, probably as a result of invasions by the Gutians and Amorites.

The Third Dynasty of Ur

For 80 years the old pattern of competing city–states returned until Ur-Nammu (r.2112–2095 BCE), the first king of the Third Dynasty of Ur, built a new empire stretching as far north as Assyria. Ur-Nammu's reign saw the construction of the first ziggurats. The Elamites sacked Ur in 2004 BCE, leading to the fall of the empire. Sumeria never regained its preeminence.

Amorite dynasties

The next 1,500 years of Mesopotamian history were dominated by Assyria and Babylon. Assyria emerged as an important trading power in the 19th century BCE and it became a major territorial power after the Amorite Shamshi-Adad took the capital Ashur, along with most of northern Mesopotamia, in about 1813 BCE. An Amorite dynasty had also set up at Babylon around

Ziggurat

A high Mesopotamian temple tower in the form of a stepped or terraced pyramid. Ziggurats were Mesopotamia's most distinctive monuments.

1894 BCE, and when Hammurabi came to the throne in 1792 BCE Babylon controlled most of Akkad (subsequently known as Babylonia). Five years later, Hammurabi conquered Sumeria. In 1781 BCE Shamshi-Adad died and most of his kingdom was under Hammurabi's control by 1757 BCE. Two years later Hammurabi conquered the last Mesopotamian power, Eshnunna. Babylon now became the religious and cultural center of Mesopotamia.

In the 17th century BCE new and threatening powers began to gather on the borders of Mesopotamia. The most important of these were the Hurrians and the Hittites. The Hurrians were a tribal people from Armenia who overran Assyria around 1680 BCE. The Hittites were an Indo-European people who had invaded Anatolia from Thrace about 1800 BCE and had emerged as a powerful kingdom by 1650 BCE. When the Hittite king Mursilis invaded and sacked Babylon in 1595 BCE, Mesopotamia entered a dark age that lasted almost two centuries. The Kassites migrated into the region from the east and by 1415 BCE Babylonia had reemerged as a Kassite kingdom.

The mechanism of government

The most notable characteristic of the early Mesopotamian empires was instability. Government was an expression of the king's will: a strong ruler could carve out an empire for himself, but if his successor were weak the empire would decline. Part of the reason for this was the mechanism of government of the empires themselves. Conquered states were not occupied, garrisoned, or subjected to a centrally controlled provincial government; instead, tribute was imposed and native rulers were given the duty of collecting and delivering it to the imperial power. This system worked well under strong emperors, but if imperial power was weakened, a vassal state could assert its independence simply by stopping payment.

Curriculum Context

In studies of the effects that new kingdoms had on the peoples of southwest Asia in the second millennium BCE, students may be asked to analyze the origins of the Hittite people in Anatolia.

Curriculum Context

The way in which emperors imposed tribute on vassal states is key to understanding the interactions between governments in early civilizations.

Hittites and Assyrians

After the Mittani kingdom
crumbled, the Hittites
became a strong power
in the Levant, successfully
defeating an invasion
by Ramesses II of Egypt
in 1285 BCE.

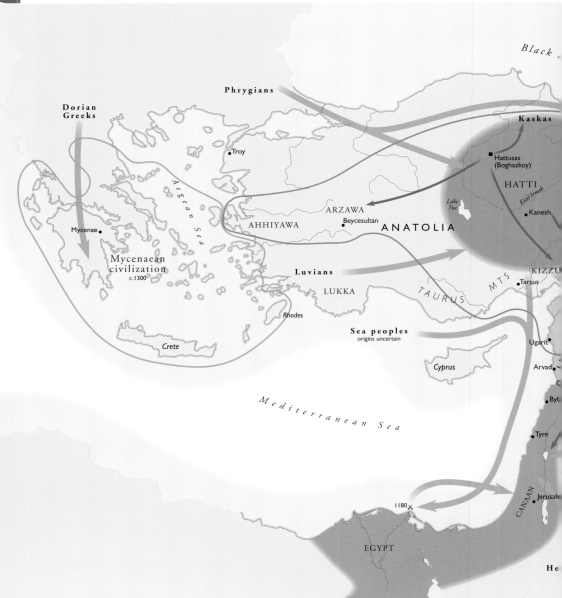

Black

Phrygians

Dorian
Greeks

Kaskas

Hattusas
(Boghazkoy)

HATTI

Troy

Lake
Tuz

Kızıl Irmak

ARZAWA

Kanesh

Aegean Sea

Beycesultan

AHHIYAWA

ANATOLIA

Mycenae

Mycenaean
civilization
c.1300

Luvians

KIZZU

LUKKA

TAURUS

MTS

Tarsus

Rhodes

Sea peoples
origins uncertain

Ugarit

Crete

Cyprus

Arvad

Mediterranean Sea

Byb

Tyre

CANAAN

1180

Jerusale

EGYPT

He

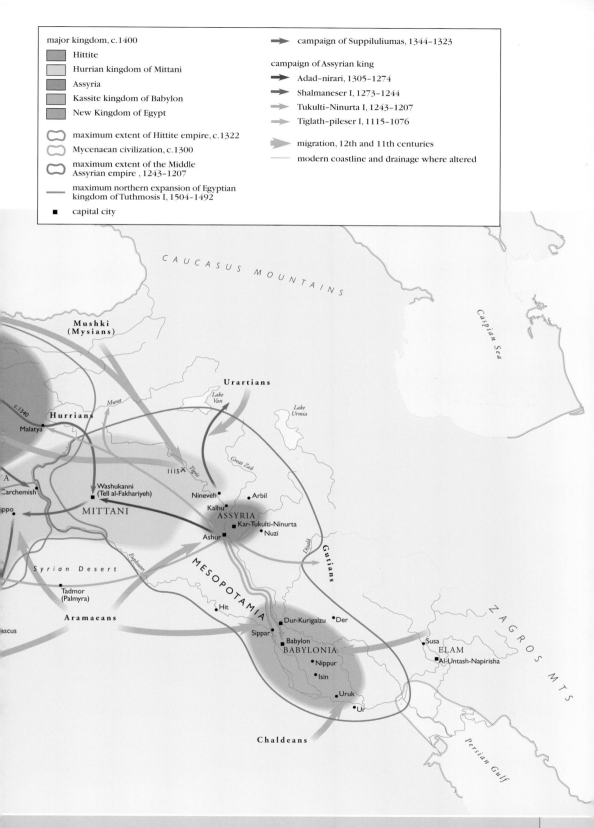

major kingdom, c.1400

Hittite

Hurrian kingdom of Mittani

Assyria

Kassite kingdom of Babylon

New Kingdom of Egypt

maximum extent of Hittite empire, c.1322

Mycenaean civilization, c.1300

maximum extent of the Middle
Assyrian empire , 1243–1207

maximum northern expansion of Egyptian
kingdom of Tuthmosis I, 1504–1492

■ capital city

campaign of Suppuluiumas, 1344–1323

campaign of Assyrian king

Adad-nirari, 1305–1274

Shalmaneser I, 1273–1244

Tukulti–Ninurta I, 1243–1207

Tiglath-pileser I, 1115–1076

migration, 12th and 11th centuries

modern coastline and drainage where altered

CAUCASUS MOUNTAINS

Caspian Sea

**Mushki
(Mysians)**

Urartians

Lake
Van

Lake
Urmia

c.1340

Hurrians

Malatya

Murat

1115

Tigris

Great Zab

A

Carchemish

Washukanni
(Tell al-Fakhariyeh)

Nineveh

Arbil

ppo

MITTANI

Kalhu

ASSYRIA

Kar-Tukulti-Ninurta

Ashur

Nuzi

Diyala

Guians

Syrian Desert

Euphrates

MESOPOTAMIA

Z
A
G
R
O
S

M
T
S

Tadmor
(Palmyra)

Aramaeans

Hit

Dur-Kurigalzu

Der

ascus

Sippar

Babylon

BABYLONIA

Susa

ELAM

Al-Untash-Napirisha

Nippur

Isin

Uruk

Ur

Chaldeans

Persian Gulf

Hittites and Assyrians

In the two centuries following the Hittite sack of Babylon in 1595 BCE, the kingdom of Mittani controlled most of northern Mesopotamia and, at its peak, southern Anatolia. Mittani was founded about 1550 BCE by the Hurrians, who had begun to encroach on northern Mesopotamia early in the previous century. As its power spread west into the Levant, Mittani came into conflict with the Egyptians.

Mittani and Egypt

Under Tuthmosis I (r.1504–1492 BCE), Egypt controlled all of the Levant and established a frontier on the Euphrates. The Egyptians were unable to maintain this frontier and over the next century Mittani regained control over the northern Levant and pushed the Egyptians south of the Orontes river.

Then, during the reign of Tuthmosis IV (r.1401–1391 BCE), Egypt and Mittani formed an alliance. The peace initiative probably came from Mittani, which was faced with a revival of Hittite power in the north while in the east the Assyrians had won back their independence. When Egypt became preoccupied with internal affairs during the reign of Akhenaten (r.1353–1335 BCE), Mittani was left exposed.

Akhenaten

The Egyptian pharaoh first known as Amenophis IV. Akhenaten tried to replace Egypt's traditional polytheism with the monotheistic cult of the Aten or sun disk.

Hittite dominance

The Hittite king Suppiluliumas (r.1344–1322 BCE) spent the early part of his reign establishing Hittite dominance in Anatolia, and then in about 1340 BCE sacked Washukanni, Mittani's capital, before sweeping on into the Levant.

Mittani began to crumble, and when Suppiluliumas launched a second campaign around 1328 BCE the western half of the kingdom fell. Suppiluliumas established a puppet ruler at Washukanni, intending

Hittite metalworkers of around 1200 BCE demonstrated their skill with this silver ceremonial drinking cup in the shape of a stag.

western Mittani to become a buffer state against Assyria. As such it was a failure, and fell to the Assyrians by 1300 BCE.

Egyptian invasion

The Hittites, who now held the same commanding position in the Levant that Mittani had held in the 15th century BCE, incurred the enmity of Egypt, where a new dynasty had come to power in 1307 BCE, eager to reestablish Egypt's position in the Levant.

By 1290 BCE the Egyptians had recovered Canaan, which had become independent under Akhenaten, and in 1285 BCE pharaoh Ramesses II (r.1290–1224 BCE) launched a major invasion of Hittite territory. The Hittite king Muwatallis II (r.1295–1271 BCE) was prepared and, in a battle between two fleets of chariots at Qadesh, Ramesses was defeated (though he claimed a great victory). The Egyptians withdrew and Hittite control was extended as far south as Damascus.

Dynasty

A succession of rulers from the same family or line.

Curriculum Context

Students learning about militarization in the second millennium BCE may be asked to give examples of chariot warfare in southwest Asia.

Relations between the two empires remained difficult until 1258 BCE, when they agreed an alliance as the Hittites were alarmed at the growth of Assyrian power.

Assyrian expansion

Assyrian expansion had begun under Ashur-uballit I (r.1363–1328 BCE), who seized Nineveh from the crumbling Mittanian kingdom in about 1330 BCE, and was continued in the 13th century BCE. Tukulti-Ninurta I (r.1243–1207 BCE) waged campaigns against the Hittites and the Kassite kingdom of Babylonia and built an empire that stretched from the upper Euphrates to the Persian Gulf. However, the empire fell apart after he was murdered by discontented nobles.

Migrations

Around 1200 BCE new waves of migrations brought chaos to the region. Shortly after 1205 BCE the Hittite kingdom collapsed, destroyed by the Phrygians, who had entered Anatolia from Thrace. At the same time Egypt came under attack from a group known to the Egyptians as the Sea Peoples.

Sea Peoples

A group of seafaring people who invaded Egypt around 1200 BCE. They may have come from the islands of the Aegean.

The origin of the Sea Peoples is uncertain. Some may have come from the Aegean islands and the Anatolian coast, but they were joined by others already settled in the Levant and Libya. They were driven from Egypt in 1180 BCE but settled in Canaan, where they became known as the Philistines. Nomadic Hebrew tribes, related to the Aramaeans, were also moving into Canaan.

Aramaean settlements in Assyria

At the end of the 12th century BCE Assyria was attacked by a confederation of Mushki (probably relatives of the Phrygians) and Anatolian peoples including the Kaskas and Hurrians. The new Assyrian king, Tiglath-pileser I (r.1115–1076 BCE), forced the invaders to retreat into Anatolia, but he had less success against the nomadic

Aramaeans who, despite 28 campaigns against them, made considerable settlements in Assyria before his death. Tiglath-pileser's successors failed to contain the Aramaeans and by 1000 BCE Assyria was reduced to its heartland around Nineveh and Ashur.

Elamite invasions of Babylon

Babylonia's main problem from the 14th to 12th centuries BCE was the kingdom of Elam. Devastating Elamite invasions of Babylon in the mid 12th century BCE led to the fall of the Kassite dynasty. Babylon recovered under a native dynasty around 1130 BCE and defeated the Elamites so thoroughly that they disappeared from history for 300 years. Then, in the 11th century BCE, Babylonia, like Assyria, had problems with migrating nomads—Aramaeans in the north, Chaldeans in the south—and, also like Assyria, was unable to do much about them. The nomads' tribal structures provided no central authority to destroy or negotiate with, and they had no cities that could be taken nor crops to be burned. The powerful Assyrian and Babylonian armies had no target to attack.

Technological advances

The period saw key technological advances, with glass, glazed pottery and bricks, and iron-smelting all appearing for the first time. Iron did not supplant bronze as the main metal for tools and weapons until around 900 BCE, but its use was widespread by 1200 BCE, the date accepted as the start of the Iron Age in the Middle East.

Curriculum Context

Some curricula may require students to examine the consequences of population movements in southwest Asia in the second millennium BCE. The settlement of nomadic Aramaeans in Assyria is a good example.

Curriculum Context

The second millennium BCE is an era during which many of the world's most fundamental technologies and techniques appeared. Students may be asked to give examples.

Assyria and Babylon

The Neo-Assyrian empire reached its peak in the eighth century BCE and the Neo-Babylonian empire was strengthened under Nebuchadnezzar in the sixth century BCE.

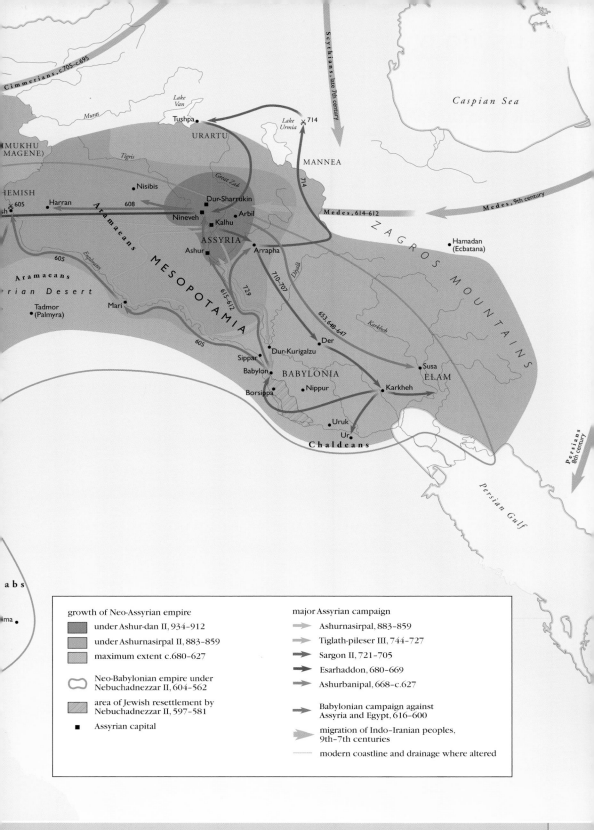

Cimmerians, c.705–c.695

Murat

Lake Van

Tushpa

URARTU

MUKHU (MAGENE)

Tigris

Nisibis

Harran   608

Dur-Sharrukin

Nineveh   Kalhu   Arbil

ASSYRIA

Ashur   Arrapha

Great Zab

Scythians, late 7th century

Lake Urmia   ✕ 714

MANNEA

714

Medes, 614–612   Medes, 9th century

Caspian Sea

Hamadan (Ecbatana)

HEMISH

605

Aramaeans

605

MESOPOTAMIA

Euphrates

615–612   729

710–707   *Diyala*

ZAGROS MOUNTAINS

Aramaeans

rian Desert

Tadmor (Palmyra)

Mari

605

653, 648–647

Der

Sippar   Dur-Kurigalzu

Babylon

Borsippa   Nippur

BABYLONIA

Karkheh

Karkheh

Susa

ELAM

Persians 8th century

Uruk

Ur

Chaldeans

Persian Gulf

modern coastline and drainage where altered

a b s

ima

growth of Neo-Assyrian empire

■ under Ashur-dan II, 934–912

■ under Ashurnasirpal II, 883–859

■ maximum extent c.680–627

Neo-Babylonian empire under Nebuchadnezzar II, 604–562

area of Jewish resettlement by Nebuchadnezzar II, 597–581

■ Assyrian capital

major Assyrian campaign

➜ Ashurnasirpal, 883–859

➜ Tiglath-pileser III, 744–727

➜ Sargon II, 721–705

➜ Esarhaddon, 680–669

➜ Ashurbanipal, 668–c.627

➜ Babylonian campaign against Assyria and Egypt, 616–600

➜ migration of Indo-Iranian peoples, 9th–7th centuries

— modern coastline and drainage where altered

Assyria and Babylon

By the 10th century BCE the Aramaeans had begun to abandon their nomadic lifestyle and to settle in city–states in the Levant and northern Mesopotamia. The Chaldeans were doing the same in southern Mesopotamia. By settling down, the Aramaeans and Chaldeans lost most of the advantages that their loose nomadic organization had given them over the old military powers.

Like the Amorites a millennium earlier, the Aramaeans and Chaldeans adopted Mesopotamian culture but the Aramaeans, at least, kept their identity; their language and alphabet was the common tongue of the region by 500 BCE. Mesopotamia experienced no further immigrations in this period, but Anatolia and Iran saw the arrival of several waves of Iranian peoples, including the Medes and the Persians, who had both formed powerful kingdoms by the sixth century BCE.

The Neo-Hittites

Of the Hittites, Assyria, and Babylon, the three powers who had dominated the region before 1200 BCE, the Hittites made the least impressive recovery. With their heartland lost to the Phrygians, the Neo-Hittites (as they are now called) formed a number of small states in southern Anatolia. They were conquered by Assyria in the eighth century BCE, after which their identity became lost.

Assyrian recovery

The Assyrian heartland around Ashur and Nineveh had survived the Aramaean invasions relatively unscathed and formed a strong base for recovery. The old pattern, established during the Middle Assyrian period, of expansion under able warrior kings followed by contraction under weak kings was continued in the new Assyrian empire. Expansion began again in the

Middle Assyrian period

The period of Assyrian expansion after Assyria regained its independence from Mitanni, around 1400 BCE. The period ended in 1076 BCE.

reign of Adad-nirari II (r.911–891 BCE) and by the reign of Ashurnasirpal II (r.883–859 BCE) the empire dominated northern Mesopotamia and received tribute from the Levant as far south as Tyre. During Ashurnasirpal's reign Ashur, Assyria's ancient capital, declined in importance and was superseded by a new purpose-built capital at Kalhu.

Curriculum Context

Students may be asked to describe the extent of the Neo-Assyrian empire and assess the sources of its wealth.

Assyrian setback in the Levant

In 854 BCE a coalition of Levantine states tried to halt the expansion of Assyrian power in the region. The coalition met Shalmaneser III (r.858–824 BCE) in battle at Qarqar on the Orontes and, although Shalmaneser claimed complete victory, Assyrian power in the Levant did suffer a setback.

Relations between Assyria and Babylon had been good since about 911 BCE, when the two states became allies. Shalmaneser gave military support to the Babylonians against the Chaldeans and also gave them assistance against internal enemies.

Decline and recovery

After Shalmaneser's reign Assyria was crippled by internal problems and went into decline for 60 years. Recovery and expansion began again in the reign of Tiglath-pileser III (r.744–727 BCE), who assumed overlordship over Babylon, reconquered the Levant, and exacted tribute from Israel and Judah.

Curriculum Context

The use of inspectors and officials in the Neo-Assyrian empire is an example of how royal bureaucracies became more effective at organizing and taxing people in the interests of the state in the first millennium BCE.

Administrative overhaul

Tiglath-pileser was responsible for a complete overhaul of the administration of the empire to assert central power. Hereditary provincial governors in the Assyrian heartlands were replaced by a hierarchy of officials under direct royal control. Traveling inspectors were sent out to examine the performance of local officials. A mail system was introduced and officials were required to send regular reports to the capital.

Vassal state

A state that is controlled by another more powerful state. Vassal states usually had to pay a tribute to the dominant state and provide military assistance when required.

Representatives were appointed to the courts of vassal states to safeguard the interests of Assyria. Large numbers of subject peoples were resettled to prevent local opposition. Finally, in perhaps the greatest break with the imperial traditions of the past, rebellious vassal states lost their nominal independence and were reorganized as provinces of Assyria, directly ruled by officials appointed by the king.

Assyrian power at its peak

Under Sargon II (r.721–705 BCE) Assyrian power reached its height. Sargon broke the power of the Armenian kingdom of Urartu and expanded Assyrian dominions with campaigns against the Chaldeans (who had seized Babylon), Elamites, and Hebrews. Sargon's last campaign ended in defeat, however, and he was killed in battle in Anatolia in 705 BCE.

Sargon's successor, Sennacherib (r.704–681 BCE), was preoccupied with rebellions in Judah, with Babylon, and with Chaldean and Elamite attacks in the south. Assyrian expansion was renewed under Esarhaddon (r.680–669 BCE), who began the conquest of Egypt, and Ashurbanipal (r.668–c.627 BCE), who completed it and took great stores of booty back to Nineveh. This last

Curriculum Context

Empire building in the first millennium BCE led to increasingly complex interrelations between the peoples of southwest Asia.

Lion hunting was symbolic to the Assyrians of royal power and only kings (Ashurbanipal in this bas-relief) were shown killing the animals.

conquest, however, succeeded only in over-extending the empire while Ashurbanipal's increasingly tyrannical rule spread discontent everywhere. Egypt regained its independence by 651 BCE and Ashurbanipal's reign ended in chaos.

Rise of Babylonian empire

The Babylonian king Nabopolassar (626–605 BCE) rebelled against Assyrian rule and after 10 years of fighting drove the Assyrians from Babylon. In 615 BCE Nabopolassar took the offensive and, supported by the Medes, took Nineveh in 612 BCE. Assyrian resistance soon ended. The Egyptian pharaoh Necho II (r.610–595 BCE) seized the opportunity offered by the collapse of Assyrian power to reoccupy the Levant, but was defeated by the Babylonian crown prince Nebuchadnezzar at Carchemish in 605 BCE.

The Babylonians followed up their victory by occupying almost all of the territory previously held by Assyria. Nebuchadnezzar came to the throne in 604 BCE and spent his reign (r.604–562 BCE) consolidating his empire, rebuilding the city of Babylon in imperial splendor and ruling within the Assyrian tradition.

Curriculum Context

Nebuchadnezzar increased the extent of the Neo-Babylonian empire, conquering Judah and Jerusalem. He is also known for his constructions, including the Hanging Gardens of Babylon.

The end of the Babylonian empire

Nebuchadnezzar's dynasty lasted only until 556 BCE, when it was overthrown in a palace coup. An official, Nabonidus (r.555–539 BCE), was chosen as king but his religious unorthodoxy soon made him unpopular in the Babylonian heartland. When the Persian king Cyrus the Great invaded in 539 BCE, Babylon surrendered without a fight, bringing to a quiet end an imperial tradition that was almost two thousand years old.

Mesopotamian civilization survived for some centuries but gradually declined under the influence of Persian, and subsequently Hellenistic, culture, and had died out by the beginning of the Christian era.

The Bible Lands

The Hebrew kingdoms of the Bible lands were dwarfed in scale and longevity by the great empires of the Middle East, yet their significance in world history is at least as great.

N

Aleppo

Neo-Hittites

Tiphsah

Orontes

Ugarit

Hamath

Syrian Desert

ARAM

Arvad

L E V A N T

Tadmor (Palmyra)

Byblos

ARAM-ZOBAH

PHOENICIA

Sidon

Damascus

ARAM-DAMASCUS

Tyre

Dan

Hazor

Acco

Sea of Chinnereth (Sea of Galilee)

Megiddo

Beth-shean

Gilboa

Mediterranean Sea

Joppa

ISRAEL AMMON

Gezer

Beth-horon

Rabbah

Baalath

Jerusalem

Gath

Salt Sea (Dead Sea)

Gaza

Hebron

PHILISTIA

MOAB

Amalekites

JUDAH

Tamar

EDOM

Ezion-geber

The Bible Lands
c.1006–965 BCE

- - - probable border of the kingdom of Saul, c.1006

kingdom of David and Solomon

—— border, 1006–928

under direct rule

vassal states and tributaries

→ campaigns of David, c.1006–965

Canaanite enclaves conquered by David

area ceded to Tyre by Solomon

fortress built by Solomon

other major building project by Solomon

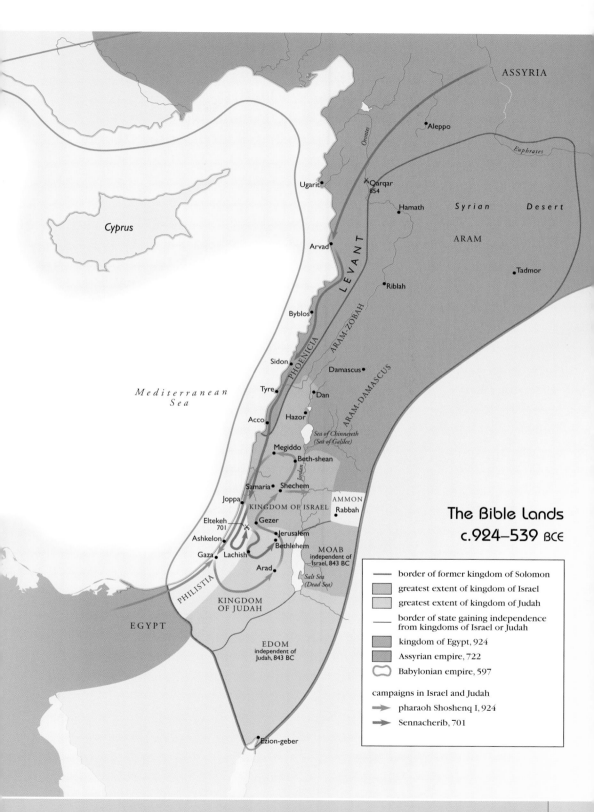

ASSYRIA

*Aleppo

*Qarqar
854

Hamath•

Syrian   Desert

ARAM

•Tadmor

Ugarit•

Orontes

Euphrates

L
E
V
A
N
T

Arvad•

Riblah•

Cyprus

Byblos•

A
R
A
M
-
Z
O
B
A
H

Mediterranean
Sea

Sidon•

Damascus•

P
H
O
E
N
I
C
I
A

Tyre•   •Dan

A
R
A
M
-
D
A
M
A
S
C
U
S

Acco•   Hazor•

Sea of Chinnereth
(Sea of Galilee)

Megiddo•

•Beth-shean

Samaria• •Shechem

Jordan

Joppa•

KINGDOM OF ISRAEL

AMMON
Rabbah•

Eltekeh
701
Ashkelon•

Gezer
•
×
•Jerusalem
•Bethlehem

MOAB
independent of
Israel, 843 BC

Gaza• •Lachish
Arad•

Salt Sea
(Dead Sea)

PHILISTIA

KINGDOM
OF JUDAH

EGYPT

EDOM
independent of
Judah, 843 BC

•Ezion-geber

The Bible Lands
c.924–539 BCE

——— border of former kingdom of Solomon

▓ greatest extent of kingdom of Israel

░ greatest extent of kingdom of Judah

——— border of state gaining independence
from kingdoms of Israel or Judah

▓ kingdom of Egypt, 924

▓ Assyrian empire, 722

◯ Babylonian empire, 597

campaigns in Israel and Judah

⟶ pharaoh Shoshenq I, 924

⟶ Sennacherib, 701

The Bible Lands

The period of the independent monarchy in the Hebrew lands, from the time of David to the Babylonian conquest in 587 BCE, was a formative time for Judaism and gave Jews a sense of historical destiny, driving them to preserve their religion and identity through centuries of foreign rule, exile, and worldwide dispersal.

The Hebrews in Canaan

The Hebrews migrated into Canaan in the early 12th century BCE. In their initial attacks under Joshua, the Hebrews occupied most of Canaan. Remaining Canaanite enclaves were mopped up in the 11th century BCE, but the Hebrews began to lose ground in the southwest to the Philistines.

Curriculum Context

Students may be asked to explain the emergence of the Jewish monarchy. The need for defense against the Philistines is an important factor.

Reign of David

The need for effective defense against the Philistines led the Hebrew tribes to unite under a monarchy. According to the Bible, the first king of the Hebrews was Saul (r.c.1020–c.1006 BCE), but it was his successor David who was responsible for consolidating the monarchy and creating the first Hebrew state. Perhaps the most important event of David's reign was his capture of Jerusalem from the Canaanite Jebusites. By making Jerusalem his capital David ensured its lasting importance as a religious center.

Curriculum Context

The reigns of David, Solomon, and Rehoboam are important in understanding the historical significance of the Hebrew kingdoms.

Reigns of Solomon and Rehoboam

David was succeeded by his son Solomon. Solomon's reign was largely peaceful, but maintaining his splendid court life and ambitious building projects, including the temple at Jerusalem, was burdensome to his people. When his successor Rehoboam (r.928–911 BCE) dealt tactlessly with the economic complaints of the northern tribes, the Hebrew kingdom split in two halves, Israel and Judah.

Revival of Assyrian power

Under Omri (r.876–869 BCE) and Ahab (r.869–850 BCE) Israel became the most powerful kingdom in the region. However, under Ahab's successor Jehu, Israel had to pay tribute to Assyria. In the eighth century BCE Tiglath-pileser III (r.744–727 BCE) overran the Levant and forced vassal status on Israel and Judah.

When Hoshea, king of Israel, rebelled against Assyria in 724 BCE his capital Samaria was taken and its population deported to Assyria. A rebellion by Hezekiah, the king of Judah, was also put down by the Assyrians. Judah briefly regained independence under Josiah (r.640–609 BCE), who extended his authority over the old kingdom of Israel until he was killed in battle with the Egyptians. The Egyptians were defeated by the Babylonians at Carchemish in 605 BCE, after which Judah became a vassal state of Babylon.

Capture of Jerusalem

In 597 BCE Judah rebelled against Babylonian rule and was crushed by Nebuchadnezzar. Jerusalem was captured and many of its citizens were deported to Babylonia. Ten years later, Judah rebelled again, but Jerusalem was taken after an 18-month siege. This was the end for independent Judah. Its last king, Zedekiah, was imprisoned and more Hebrews were deported. Many others fled into exile in Egypt.

Curriculum Context

Many curricula require students to assess the significance of the Babylonian captivity and analyze how the Jews maintained religious and cultural traditions despite the destruction of the Hebrew kingdoms.

Babylonian captivity

Although a disaster in political terms, the Babylonian captivity was a creative period in Jewish history. Exile caused a great deal of religious reflection and this was the period when much of the Old Testament was written up in something close to its present form. Nor in many ways were the conditions of the exile too harsh. When Cyrus the Great of Persia destroyed the Babylonian empire in 539 BCE and gave the Jews leave to return home, thousands chose to remain where they were. Many others remained in Egypt. It was the beginning of the Diaspora.

Achemenid Persia

The formation of the Achemenid Persian empire began in 550 BCE under Cyrus the Great. It became the largest empire the ancient world had seen.

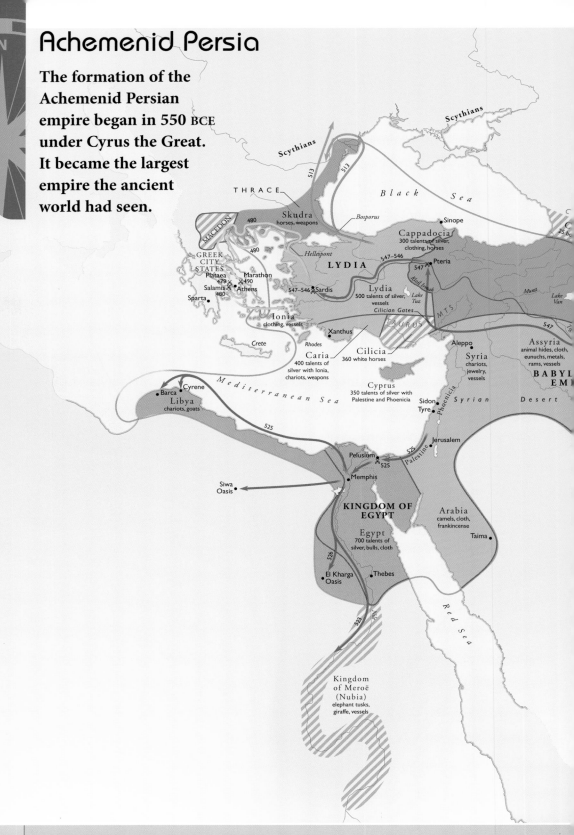

Scythians

Scythians

THRACE

Black   *Sea*

MACEDON

480

Skudra
horses, weapons

Bosporus

Sinope

Cappadocia
300 talents of silver,
clothing, horses

GREEK
CITY
STATES

480

Hellespont

LYDIA

547–546

547 Pteria

25 b

Plataea
479

Marathon
490

Kızıl Irmak

Munit

Lake
Van

Salamis
480

Athens

547–546 Sardis

Lydia
500 talents of silver,
vessels

Lake
Tuz

MTS

547

Sparta

Ionia
clothing, vessels

Cilician Gates

TAURUS

Assyria
animal hides, cloth,
eunuchs, metals,
rams, vessels

Xanthus

Crete

Rhodes

Caria
400 talents of
silver with Ionia,
chariots, weapons

Cilicia
360 white horses

Aleppo

Syria
chariots,
jewelry,
vessels

BABYL
EM

Mediterranean   Sea

Cyprus
350 talents of silver with
Palestine and Phoenicia

Sidon

Syrian   *Desert*

Barca

Cyrene

525

Libya
chariots, goats

Tyre

Phoenicia

Jerusalem

525

Pelusium

525

Palestine

Siwa
Oasis

Memphis

KINGDOM OF
EGYPT

Arabia
camels, cloth,
frankincense

526

Egypt
700 talents of
silver, bulls, cloth

Taima

El Kharga
Oasis

Thebes

Red   Sea

523

Kingdom
of Meroë
(Nubia)
elephant tusks,
giraffe, vessels

Achemenid Persia

The Persians who took Babylon in 539 BCE were comparative newcomers to the region. An Indo-Iranian people, they had followed their close relations the Medes from central Asia to Iran in the eighth century. The founder of the Persian monarchy was Achemenes, who gave his name to the dynasty, but it is uncertain when he ruled. It was during the reign of Cyrus the Great (r.559–529 BCE) that Persia rose to empire.

The empire under Cyrus the Great

Cyrus' career as a great conqueror started when his nominal overlord, the Median king Astyages, invaded Persia around 550 BCE. Astyages was captured when he met Cyrus in battle at Pasargadae. Cyrus followed up this easy victory by taking the Median capital at Hamadan (Ecbatana). Cyrus was now the most powerful ruler in the region.

Curriculum Context

Students learning about the development of the Persian empire may be asked to describe the victories of Cyrus the Great against the Medes, Lydians, and Ionian Greeks.

In 547 BCE Cyrus repulsed an invasion of Media by King Croesus of Lydia. Cyrus then took the Lydian capital Sardis. Leaving his generals to complete the conquest of Lydia and the Ionian Greeks, Cyrus marched into central Asia. In 539 BCE he conquered Babylonia.

In little more than a decade Cyrus had built the largest empire the world had yet seen, with remarkably little hard fighting. Consolidation of his empire owed much to his moderation. His demands for tribute were modest, he did not interfere with local customs and left local institutions of government intact.

Cyrus was killed in 530 BCE on a campaign against the Sakas in central Asia. He was succeeded by his son Cambyses, who added Egypt and Libya to the empire. He was succeeded by his brother Smerdis, who was quickly overthrown and killed by Darius (r.521–486 BCE), a member of a junior Achemenid house.

The empire under Darius

Darius faced rebellions from one end of the empire to the other but suppressed them all within a year. By 520 BCE he was secure enough to campaign against the Caspian Scythians. In 518 BCE he extended Persian control as far as, and possibly a little beyond, the Indus and in 513 BCE he crossed into Europe; although he conquered Thrace, the expedition failed in its main objective of subduing the Black Sea Scythians.

This failure encouraged a rebellion by the Ionian Greeks in 499 BCE. This was put down in 494 BCE and Darius dispatched an expedition to punish the mainland Greeks for supporting the rebels. When this force was defeated by the Athenians at the Battle of Marathon in 490 BCE, Darius began to plan for the conquest of Greece. The expedition was finally launched by his son Xerxes, but the decisive defeat of his fleet at Salamis in 480 BCE and of his army at Plataea the following year brought the expansion of the empire to a halt.

Imperial administration

Darius reorganized the empire into about 20 provinces under satraps, often relatives or close friends of the king. The system of taxation was regularized and fixed tributes were introduced. Only Persia, which was not a conquered province, was exempt. The Assyrian imperial mail system was expanded and the roads improved. The official capital of the empire under Cyrus had been Pasargadae, but Hamadan was effectively the administrative capital. Darius moved the administrative capital to Susa and founded a new official capital at Persepolis. Under Darius the imperial administration used various local languages transcribed into cuneiform and written on clay tablets for documents, but his successors abandoned this system in favor of writing on parchment using the widespread Aramaic language and alphabet.

Ancient Egypt: Middle and New Kingdoms

The period known as the Middle Kingdom began in 2040 BCE, when Egypt was reunified under one ruler based at Thebes.

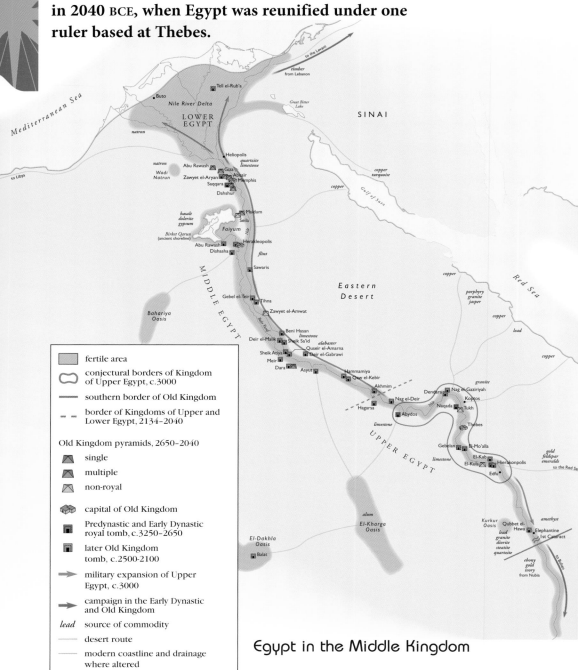

Egypt in the Middle Kingdom

fertile area

conjectural borders of Kingdom of Upper Egypt, c.3000

southern border of Old Kingdom

border of Kingdoms of Upper and Lower Egypt, 2134–2040

Old Kingdom pyramids, 2650–2040

single

multiple

non-royal

capital of Old Kingdom

Predynastic and Early Dynastic royal tomb, c.3250–2650

later Old Kingdom tomb, c.2500-2100

military expansion of Upper Egypt, c.3000

campaign in the Early Dynastic and Old Kingdom

lead source of commodity

desert route

modern coastline and drainage where altered

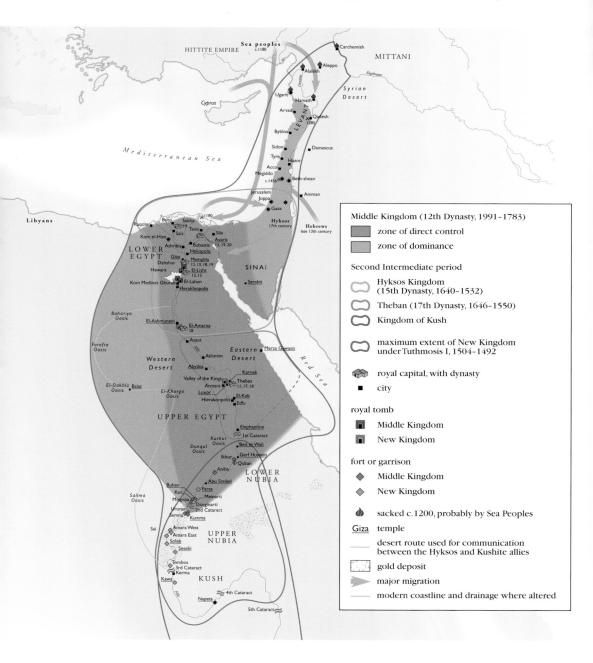

Egypt in the New Kingdom

HITTITE EMPIRE
Sea peoples c.1180
Carchemish
MITTANI
Aleppo
Alalakh
Euphrates
Ugarit
Hamath
Syrian Desert
Cyprus
Arvad
Qadesh 1285
Byblos
Mediterranean Sea
Sidon
Damascus
Tyre
Hazor
Acco
Megiddo c.1456
Beth-shean
Jerusalem
Joppa
Amman
Gaza
Libyans
1180
Raqote
Buto
Sakha
Hyksos 17th century
Hebrews late 13th century
Kom el-Hisn
Sais
Sile
Tanis
Avaris
Athribis
Bubastis 15, 19, 20
LOWER EGYPT
Giza
Heliopolis
SINAI
Dahshur
Memphis 12, 13, 18, 19
Hawara
El-Lisht 12, 13
Kom Medinet Ghurab
El-Lahun
Serabit
Herakleopolis
Bahariya Oasis
El-Ashmunein
El-Amarna 18
Farafra Oasis
Asyut
Eastern Desert
Mersa Gawasis
Akhmim
Western Desert
Abydos
Red Sea
El-Dakhla Oasis
Balat
Valley of the Kings
Thebes 11, 17, 18
El-Kharga Oasis
Armant
Luxor
El-Kab
Hierakonpolis
Edfu
UPPER EGYPT
Elephantine
Kurkur Oasis
1st Cataract
Beit el-Wali
Dunqul Oasis
Ikkur
Gerf Hussein
Quban
Aniba
LOWER NUBIA
Abu Simbel
Salima Oasis
Buhen
Kor
Faras
Mirgissa
Meinarti
Uronarti
Dorginarti
Semna
2nd Cataract
Sai
Kumma
Amara West
Amara East
UPPER NUBIA
Soleb
Sesebi
Tombos
3rd Cataract
Kerma
Kawa
KUSH
4th Cataract
Napata
5th Cataract

Middle Kingdom (12th Dynasty, 1991–1783)

- zone of direct control
- zone of dominance

Second Intermediate period

- Hyksos Kingdom (15th Dynasty, 1640–1532)
- Theban (17th Dynasty, 1646–1550)
- Kingdom of Kush
- maximum extent of New Kingdom under Tuthmosis I, 1504–1492
- royal capital, with dynasty
- ■ city

royal tomb

- Middle Kingdom
- New Kingdom

fort or garrison

- ◆ Middle Kingdom
- ◆ New Kingdom
- 🔥 sacked c.1200, probably by Sea Peoples
- <u>Giza</u> temple
- desert route used for communication between the Hyksos and Kushite allies
- gold deposit
- ➤ major migration
- modern coastline and drainage where altered

Ancient Egypt: Middle and New Kingdoms

The reunification of Egypt in 2040 BCE by Mentuhotpe (r.2061–2010 BCE), of the Theban dynasty of Upper Egypt, marks the start of the Middle Kingdom. A few decades later royal authority and political stability had been restored and the power of the provincial governors reduced.

Old Kingdom

The period of Egyptian history (c.2575–2134 BCE) when Egypt achieved its first high point of civilization. The Old Kingdom is sometimes referred to as "the Age of the Pyramids."

Vizier

A high-ranking political official or advisor.

To rebuild a loyal administration, the Middle Kingdom rulers promoted propagandist literature, while statuary presented the king as the careworn "good shepherd" of his people. Pyramid building was revived, though more modestly than in the Old Kingdom.

Extension of Egyptian influence

Egypt's neighbors were now becoming organized in chiefdoms and petty kingdoms, and the Middle Kingdom rulers had to pursue a more aggressive foreign policy than their predecessors. Under Amenemhet I (r.1991–1962 BCE), Lower Nubia was conquered; the frontier at the Second Cataract was garrisoned and heavily fortified by his successors. Egyptian influence was extended over the Levant during the reign of Senwosret III (r.1878–1841 BCE).

During the 18th century BCE the bureaucracy began to grow out of control and for much of the time the effective rulers of Egypt were the viziers. In the 17th century BCE there was considerable immigration from the Levant into the Delta. Most immigrants were absorbed into the lower classes of Egyptian society but one, Khendjer, became king around 1745 BCE.

Invasion by the Hyksos

Around 1640 BCE Egypt was invaded by the Hyksos, a Semitic people from the Levant, who overran Lower

Egypt, which they ruled from their capital at Avaris in the Delta. Upper Egypt remained independent under a vassal Theban dynasty, but control over Lower Nubia was lost to the nascent kingdom of Kush.

Hyksos rule, in what is known as the Second Intermediate period, made Egypt more open to foreign influences. Bronze came into widespread use and war chariots were introduced, as were weapons such as the composite bow and scale armor. New fashions in dress, musical instruments, domestic animals, and crops were adopted through Hyksos influence. Otherwise, the Hyksos accepted Egyptian traditions and historical continuity was unbroken.

The New Kingdom

Under the Theban king Seqenenre II (died c.1555 BCE) the Egyptians began a long struggle to expel the Hyksos, which was finally completed by Ahmose in 1532 BCE. This victory marks the beginning of the New Kingdom, under which the power and influence of ancient Egypt reached its peak.

The Hyksos invasion had shown the Egyptians that their borders were no longer secure, and the New Kingdom was overtly militaristic and expansionist, reaching its greatest extent around 1500 BCE under the warrior king Tuthmosis I. Tuthmosis conquered the entire Levant and established a frontier on the Euphrates. Lower Nubia was reconquered and Kush was overrun to beyond the Fourth Cataract.

The primary motive of expansion into the Levant was to establish a buffer zone between Egypt and the aggressive powers of the Middle East; in Nubia, which had rich gold deposits, the motive was economic. In the Levant, local rulers were kept under the supervision of Egyptian officials and key cities were garrisoned. Nubia was subjected to full colonial

Curriculum Context

Students learning about the Egyptian civilization may be asked to describe the technological advances made during the second millennium BCE, including the use of bronze, weapons, and luxury goods.

Curriculum Context

In a study of the New Kingdom, students may be required to explain the spread of Egyptian power into Nubia and southwest Asia and assess the motives for expansion.

government under a viceroy directly responsible to the king. Nubia was a great source of wealth to the New Kingdom, but the Egyptians faced a constant struggle to keep control of the Levant against local rebellions and expansionist powers such as the Hittite empire.

Changes under Akhenaten

The power of Egypt declined after the reign of Amenophis IV (r.1353–1335 BCE). Amenophis, who changed his name to Akhenaten, was a radical religious reformer who attempted to replace Egypt's traditional polytheism with the monotheistic cult of the Aten or sun disk. Akhenaten founded a new capital and promoted radically new art styles to symbolize the break with the past, but there was little popular enthusiasm for the new religion, which was abandoned after his death.

Curriculum Context

Students may be required to describe the religious ideas of Akhenaten and assess the cult of the Aten as an early form of monotheism.

War chariots and the powerful composite bow were introduced to Egypt by the Hyksos. This painting of the boy-king Tutankhamun portrays him using both.

Political instability

In the ensuing period of political instability, Egypt lost control of the Levant to the Hittites. Campaigns by the kings (or pharaohs as they were now known) Sethos I (r.1305–1290 BCE) and Ramesses II "the Great" (r.1290–1224 BCE) to restore the Egyptian position were only partially successful, and Ramesses eventually made peace with the Hittites.

Around 1200 BCE the entire region was disrupted by waves of migrations. In the 1180s BCE Egypt was invaded by the Sea Peoples, a coalition of Aegean, Anatolian, and Levantine peoples. They were driven off after a naval battle in the Delta by Ramesses III, but he could not prevent them settling around Gaza.

During the New Kingdom large tracts of land were granted to the temples, and by the 11th century BCE they controlled a third of Egyptian land: the temple of Amun at Karnak effectively controlled all Upper Egypt. By now the priesthood had become hereditary and was largely out of the king's direct control.

The Third Intermediate period

The Third Intermediate period (1070–712 BCE) was a period of weak monarchies and decentralized power. The empire of the New Kingdom was completely lost by 1000 BCE. Although the petty kingdoms of the Levant posed no threat to Egypt, the Nubian kingdom of Kush developed into a powerful Egyptianate state which eventually conquered Egypt in 712 BCE.

The Late period

The Nubian conquest marked the beginning of the Late period (712–332 BCE) which saw foreign influence in, and over, Egypt increase. Spells of Nubian, Assyrian, and Persian rule were followed by revivals under native dynasties, but after the conquest by Alexander the Great in 332 BCE Egypt was under foreign rule.

Curriculum Context

The migrations of the Sea Peoples are key to understanding the importance of population movements in the second millennium BCE.

Neolithic Europe

The first farming in Europe began in Greece and the Balkans around 6500 BCE. As farming spread to central and northern Europe, more complex hierarchical settlements emerged.

N

Ring of Brodgar
Skara Brae
Maes Howe
Callanish
Orkney Islands
Camster Long
Clava
Monamore
Ballynagilly
Castlerigg
Carrowmore
Long Meg & Daughters
Newgrange
The Knowth
Great Langdale
Bryncelli Ddu
Lough Gur
Barclodiadd y Gawres
Derrynahinch
Belas Knap
Emmen
Mynydd-bach
Rollright
Havelte
Ty Isaf
Stones
Elsloo
Windmill Hill
Avebury
Langweiler
Stonehenge
Köln-Lindenthal
Merry Maidens
La Chausée-
Weris
Tirancourt
Les Fouaillages
La Hogue
Michelsberg
Barnenez
Tressé
Aillevans
Liscuis
Noisy
Carnac
Cortaillod
Gavrinis
Chassey
Sion
Puy de
Lagozza
Paulhiac
Arene Candide
St.Michel-
La Halliade
du-Touch
Pedra Coberta
Pouey-
Mayou
Perarine
Corsica
Artajona
Settiva
Puig Roig
Fontanaccia
Li Muri
Carapito
Els Tudons
Sardinia
Anta da Marquesa
Furninha
Cabeço da
Balearic
Arruda
Poço da Gateira
Islands
Pedra Branca
Anta dos Gorgions
Nora Velha
Dolmen de Soto
Alcalá
Los Millares
Cueva de la Menga
Romeral
Romeral
El Barranquete
Dougga
Los Murcielagos
Bou Nouara
Kristel-Jardins
Gar Cahal

Väve
Häg
Ålborg
Jordhøj
Spanskhøj
Tustrup
Grønhøj
Toftum
Sarup
Gr
Liepen
Olde
Altendorf
Danub
Po
Rhine
Rhône
ALPS
Loire
Douro
Tagus
PYRENEES

ATLANTIC
OCEAN

earliest farming cultures

- early Aegean and Anatolian Painted Ware cultures, 7000–6000
- Balkan Painted and Impressed Pottery cultures, 6500–4000
- Impressed Pottery cultures, 6000–4000
- Bandkeramik or Linear Pottery culture, 5400–4500
- Bowl cultures, 4500–3300
- Tripolye–Cucuteni cultures, 4200–3800
- Funnel-necked Beaker cultures, 4200–2800

- megalithic monument building, 4300–2000
- stone circle or alignment
- megalithic tomb
- ≈ excavation of early farming village
- • other site
- ······· spread of copper working by 4500
- ········ spread of copper working by 3000
- → general direction of the spread of farming, 6000–3000

Vättern

Lake Peipus

Western Dvina

Ramshög

kers Høj

Vistula

nkau

Olszanice

Oder

Bylany

Tripolye

Dnieper

C A R P A T H I A N S

Habasesti

Hódmezővásárhely

Cucuteni

Tartaria

Varna

Sava

Vinca

Danube

Starcevo

Rudna Glava

Karanovo

B l a c k   S e a

Sitagroi

Coppa Nevigata

A N A T O L I A

Argissa

Hagia Gala

Beycesultan
Hacilar

Frankhthi

Stentinello

M e d i t e r r a n e a n   S e a

Crete

Knossos

Cyprus

Tarxien

Neolithic Europe

The spread of agriculture through Europe was a complex process of small-scale migrations by farming peoples and the adoption of farming techniques by indigenous hunter–gatherers. It took time to develop crop strains that were suited to the colder and wetter climates of central, western, and northern Europe.

Hunter-gatherers readily adopted some aspects of the material culture of neighboring farmers, such as pottery and polished stone axes, but only adopted food production when natural food sources were in short supply. In many areas, Mesolithic hunter–gatherers were already semi-sedentary, so the transition to a settled farming way of life was probably easily made when it became necessary.

The beginning of farming in Europe

Farming, based on cereals, legumes, sheep, goats, and cattle, first began in Europe in Greece and the Balkans around 6500 BCE. This pattern of farming spread from the Balkans around the Mediterranean coasts to southern France and Spain by 5000 BCE. Whether the adoption of farming was an indigenous development or was influenced by the farming societies of the Middle East is doubtful. Southeastern Europe was within the range of wild einkorn wheat, cattle, pigs, and sheep, and farming may have developed as a result of experimentation with cultivation and animal husbandry by indigenous hunter–gatherers. Cattle may have been domesticated independently in southeast Europe but some crops, such as emmer wheat and barley, were certainly introduced from the Middle East.

The earliest farming culture of central Europe is the Bandkeramik or Linear Pottery culture. This originated in the northern Balkans around 5400 BCE and over a few centuries spread north and west across the band of fertile and easily worked loess soils that extends across Europe from Romania to the Rhineland. When the population of a village became too large, a daughter settlement was simply founded a few miles away. The indigenous Mesolithic hunter–gatherer bands were not displaced by the Bandkeramik people, who settled on vacant lands between them, usually along rivers.

However, steady encroachment by the farmers placed pressure on the hunter–gatherers' resources, and they were gradually forced to adopt farming too: gradually the two populations became assimilated. After a delay of several centuries, the farming way of life spread from central Europe into western Europe, then Britain and Scandinavia and the southwest steppes.

Farming in central and northern Europe

Farming in central and northern Europe was very different from that in the south. The cold winters led to spring sowing of crops (autumn sowing prevailed in southern Europe, the Middle East, and north Africa) and there was greater emphasis on cattle and pigs, which were better suited to grazing in woodland than sheep and goats.

Neolithic settlements

Neolithic settlements were generally small, with populations of only 40 to 60. The most common type of building was the wooden longhouse that accommodated both people and livestock. Except in treeless areas such as the Orkney Islands, where stone houses were built, settlements have left few traces.

Burials and ritual structures provide most evidence of the nature of Neolithic societies. In most of Europe the dead were buried in individual graves in cemeteries with grave goods of stone tools, ornaments, and pottery. There is little variation in the quantity and

Curriculum Context

The spread of the Bandkeramik culture was influenced by Europe's soils. The curriculum may ask students to show how the shape of early communities reflected local conditions.

Grave goods

Objects left with the body of a dead person at the time of burial or cremation. Examples included personal possessions of the deceased, textiles, weapons, pottery, and jewelry.

quality of grave goods, indicating that these communities were egalitarian. In many areas of western Europe the dead were buried communally in megalithic tombs which remained in use for many generations. The tombs were usually covered with mounds of earth and they may have served as territorial markers as well as burial places, the presence of the community's ancestors legitimizing the ownership of the present generation.

The Atlantic coast of western Europe, where the earliest megalithic tombs were built, was already relatively densely populated in Mesolithic times. Population pressure may have been felt after the introduction of agriculture, leading to a new concern with territoriality.

Bell Beaker drinking cups with incised decoration have been found in graves all over western Europe. Pollen grains found in the bottom of some indicate that they had contained a mead-like drink.

Megalithic stone circles

In the later Neolithic and the early Bronze Age, northwest Europe saw the construction of megalithic stone circles and circular earth structures known as henges. Some circles have astronomical alignments or form part of a complex ritual landscape but their exact functions are unknown. Some monuments are so large that they must have been built by chiefdoms able to command the resources and populations of wide areas.

Later Neolithic burial practices

The emergence of more hierarchical societies in the later Neolithic is also reflected in burial practices. In cultures such as the Cord Impressed Ware culture of eastern Europe and the Bell Beaker cultures in western Europe, variations in the quality and quantity of grave goods in burials indicate differences of wealth and status in farming societies. In many areas these changes are associated with the introduction of copper and gold metallurgy.

Metallurgy developed separately in the northern Balkans around 4800 BCE and in southern Spain about 15 centuries later. Both copper and gold were used to make tools and ornaments. At first only native metals were used, but by 4500 BCE copper ores were being mined in the Balkans for smelting. Copper was smelted in Spain, Italy, and probably Britain by 2400 BCE. Copper tools had few advantages over stone ones, but the elites valued metal for display objects. Only in the Bronze Age did metal tools begin to replace stone tools in everyday use.

Curriculum Context

Students may be asked to assess how megalithic stone circles and henges are evidence of the emergence of hierarchical agrarian societies.

Curriculum Context

Burial sites are an important source of archeological evidence in understanding the characteristics of Neolithic societies such as the Bell Beaker culture.

Curriculum Context

The use of metals such as copper for functional and nonfunctional purposes is key to understanding the cultural and technological achievements of the later Neolithic period.

Bronze Age Europe

The Bronze Age in Europe began in the late third millennium BCE. The period saw the rise of a warrior class and increased long-distance trade.

Jarlshof
Shetland Islands

sub-Neolithic forest hunters and gatherers

Rickeby
Hallunda
Vänern
Vättern
Tromøy
Kvarnby

Memsie

Bulbjerg

Trundholm
Brudevaelte
Egtved
Kivik
Voldtofte

Downpatrick
Staple Howe
Perleberg
Biskupin
Janko
Kam
Knocknalappa
Dinorben
Mam Tor
Fengate
Drenthe
Barger-Oosterveld
Nieder-Neundorf
Island
Brenig
Schweinert
Miejsce
Irthlingborough
Ram's Hill
Toterfout
Leubingen
Grossenheim
Bush Barrow
Court St Etienne
Helmsdorf
Trethellan
Stonehenge
Bad Nauheim
Velatice
Blackpatch
Gedinne
Flörsheim
Postoloprty
Langdon-Bay
Havré
Heidesheim
Unetice
Salcombe
Blucina
Veterov
Aulnay-aux-Planches
Hagenam
Mannheim
Kernonen
Fort
Danube
Kelheim
Unter-Radl
Harrouard
Wasserburg
Ettins
Nitriansky Hrádok
Vál
Rixheim
Baldegg
Volders
Caka
Loire
Hölting
Ptuj
Kisap
Wittnauer Horn
Cortaillod
Ledro
Bled
Crestaulta
Angarano
Dobova
Sava
Polada
ATLANTIC
Canegrate
OCEAN
Fontanella
Mailhac
Bismantora
Agullana
Luni
Corsica
Cortes de
Can Missert
Allumiere
Navarra
Filitosa
Narce
Ebro
Douro
Nuraghe
El Molá
Albucci
Phlegraean
Scoglio del
Tagus
San Carla
Fields
Tonno
Ses Paisses
Barumini
Balearic
Sardinia
Islands
Lipara
El Officio
Millazzo
Cerro de
Real
Sicily
Huelva
El Argar
Borg in-Nadur
Malta

Rhine
Elbe
Oder
Vistu
Seine
ALPS
Rhône

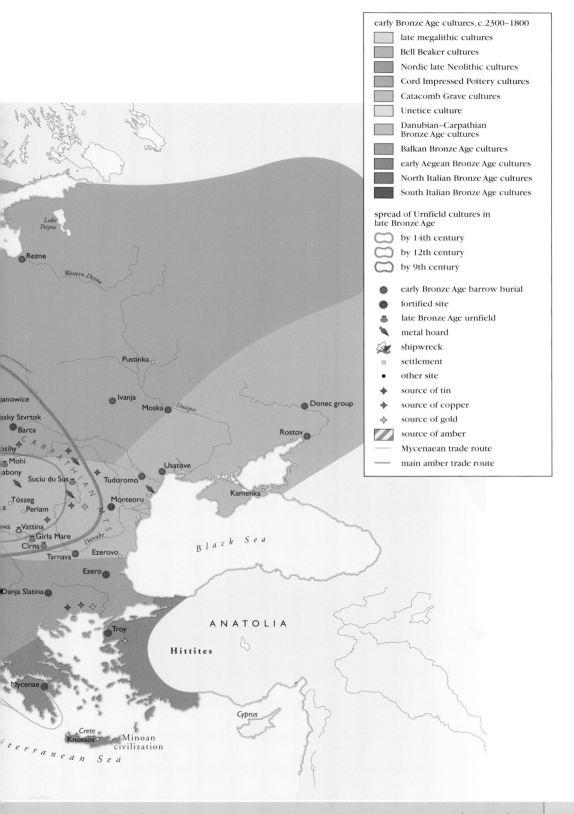

early Bronze Age cultures, c.2300–1800

- late megalithic cultures
- Bell Beaker cultures
- Nordic late Neolithic cultures
- Cord Impressed Pottery cultures
- Catacomb Grave cultures
- Unetice culture
- Danubian–Carpathian Bronze Age cultures
- Balkan Bronze Age cultures
- early Aegean Bronze Age cultures
- North Italian Bronze Age cultures
- South Italian Bronze Age cultures

spread of Urnfield cultures in late Bronze Age

- by 14th century
- by 12th century
- by 9th century

- early Bronze Age barrow burial
- fortified site
- late Bronze Age urnfield
- metal hoard
- shipwreck
- settlement
- other site
- source of tin
- source of copper
- source of gold
- source of amber
- Mycenaean trade route
- main amber trade route

Lake Peipus

Rezne

Western Dvina

Pustinka

Ivanja

Moska

Dnieper

Donec group

Rostov

Usatove

Kamenka

anowice

ssky Stvrtok

Barca

osihy

Mohi

abony

Suciu du Sus

Tudoromo

Tószeg

Periam

Monteoru

va

Vattina

Girla Mare

Cirna

Tarnava

Ezerovo

Danube

Black Sea

Ezero

Danja Slatina

C A R P A T H I A N   M T S

Troy

Hittites

A N A T O L I A

Mycenae

Cyprus

Crete

Knossos

Minoan civilization

terranean   Sea

Bronze Age Europe

The Bronze Age saw chiefdoms and warrior elites established across most of Europe. Beyond the Aegean, states were not formed until the Iron Age was well advanced and in northern and eastern Europe not until the early Middle Ages.

Bronze Age chiefdoms were competitive communities: fortifications were built in great numbers and new weapons such as swords and halberds were invented. Superbly crafted display objects made of bronze and precious metals—ornaments, weapons, "parade-ground" armor, tableware, and cult objects—express the competitiveness of the period.

Long-distance trade

Long-distance trade, particularly in tin and amber, arose to satisfy the demand for metals and other precious objects in areas where such resources were lacking. The increase in long-distance trade aided the spread of ideas and fashions and led to a high degree of cultural uniformity.

The Bronze Age in Europe

The earliest-known use of bronze in Europe, in the Unetice culture in central Europe about 2500 BCE, was probably an independent development and not the result of influence from the Middle East.

Bronze came into use in southeast Europe, the Aegean, and Italy 200 years later, followed by Spain and, finally, the British Isles in about 1800 BCE. Scandinavia, with no workable deposits of copper or tin, continued in the Stone Age until the middle of the second millennium BCE. By this time bronze had entered Scandinavia, brought by traders in exchange for amber and, probably, furs.

Curriculum Context

The development of long-distance trade is key to the emergence of increasingly complex societies in Europe.

Metal technology

Bronze technology led to a rapid increase in the use of metals. Bronze weapons and tools kept an edge better than stone or copper, could easily be resharpened, and when broken could be melted down and recast. It was expensive, however, and its use was largely confined to the social elites in the early Bronze Age.

Stone tools, sometimes copying the style of prestigious bronze tools, continued in everyday use. Large quantities of bronze artifacts, often of the highest quality, were buried or sunk in bogs as offerings to the gods.

Bronze Age burials

The social distinctions of Bronze Age society are apparent in burial practices. A minority of burials are richly furnished with grave goods but the majority have few offerings.

In the earlier Bronze Age three distinct burial practices are found. In southeast Europe the normal practice was burial of rich and poor alike in flat grave cemeteries. In most of eastern, northern, and western Europe the poor were buried in flat graves but the rich were buried under barrows. In some parts of western Europe Neolithic-style communal burials in megalithic tombs continued until about 1200 BCE.

Settlement patterns

In southern and central Europe, large villages, often fortified, developed but in northern and western Europe the settlement pattern was one of dispersed homesteads. Population rose across Europe and agricultural settlers moved into many marginal upland areas. These were abandoned late in the Bronze Age, perhaps because of climatic deterioration or because the poor soils had been exhausted. As agricultural land rose in value, clear boundaries were laid out between

Curriculum Context

The curriculum may ask students to assess the uses and significance of bronze tools, weapons, and luxury goods in the Bronze Age period.

Barrow

An ancient burial mound consisting of a large mound of earth or stones placed over a burial site.

Votive offerings thrown into bogs include this bronze and gold "chariot of the sun" from Trundholm (Denmark).

Curriculum Context

The introduction of improved plow technology is an important factor in the development of agrarian settlements in Europe.

communities in many areas, especially northwest Europe, and farmland was enclosed into small fields that could be managed more intensively. Farmers benefited from the introduction of heavier plows, wheeled vehicles, and horses. European wild oats were domesticated at this time, probably as horse fodder.

The Urnfield culture

Around 1350 BCE the Urnfield culture, named for its distinctive burial practices, appeared in Hungary.

Bodies were cremated and the ashes buried in funerary urns in flat grave cemeteries of hundreds, even thousands, of graves. As with earlier Bronze Age burial customs, a minority of graves included rich offerings, weapons, and armor. Some of these graves were covered with barrows, demonstrating a degree of continuity with the past, but this was by no means universal: the powers enjoyed by chieftains in the early Bronze Age may have been undermined to an extent by the emergence of a warrior class.

By the ninth century BCE Urnfield customs had spread over most of continental Europe. Except in the west, where it was probably taken by migrating Celtic peoples, the Urnfield culture spread mainly as a result of the wide-ranging contacts on trade links.

The later Bronze Age

The later Bronze Age saw increased militarization, with extensive fortress building in western Europe and the introduction of the bronze slashing sword. Bronze armor was introduced, but probably for display only: it offers less protection than leather.

Small numbers of iron artifacts appeared in many areas about 1200 BCE. However, iron tools first became common only around 1000 BCE in Greece and 250 years later in northern Europe.

Curriculum Context

Burial practices are important in providing archeological evidence for the social organization of Bronze Age settlements. Barrows required communal effort to build and are evidence of the power of the elites.

First Civilizations in the Mediterranean

By 2000 BCE Europe's first urban civilization was flourishing in Crete. It lasted until 1450 BCE when the Mycenaean culture became dominant.

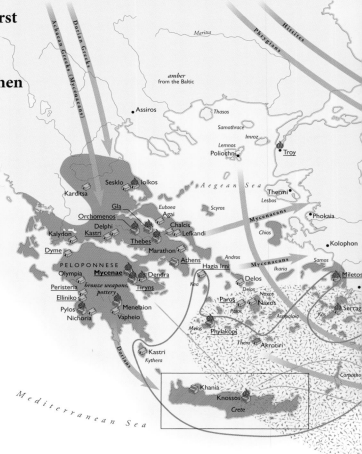

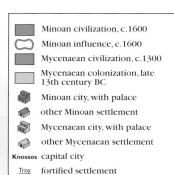

Minoan civilization, c.1600	site damaged or destroyed by invaders from the north, or "Sea Peoples", c.1200
Minoan influence, c.1600	mountain-top shrine on Crete
Mycenaean civilization, c.1300	sacred cave on Crete
Mycenaean colonization, late 13th century BC	shipwreck
Minoan city, with palace	probable trading route of the Ulu Burun ship
other Minoan settlement	*ivory* source of objects in the cargo of the Ulu Burun wreck, 14th century BC
Mycenaean city, with palace	major migration, c.2000
other Mycenaean settlement	major migration, c.1200
Knossos capital city	area affected by ash falls from the eruption of Thera, 1626
Troy fortified settlement	
site damaged or destroyed by Mycenaeans, c.1450	

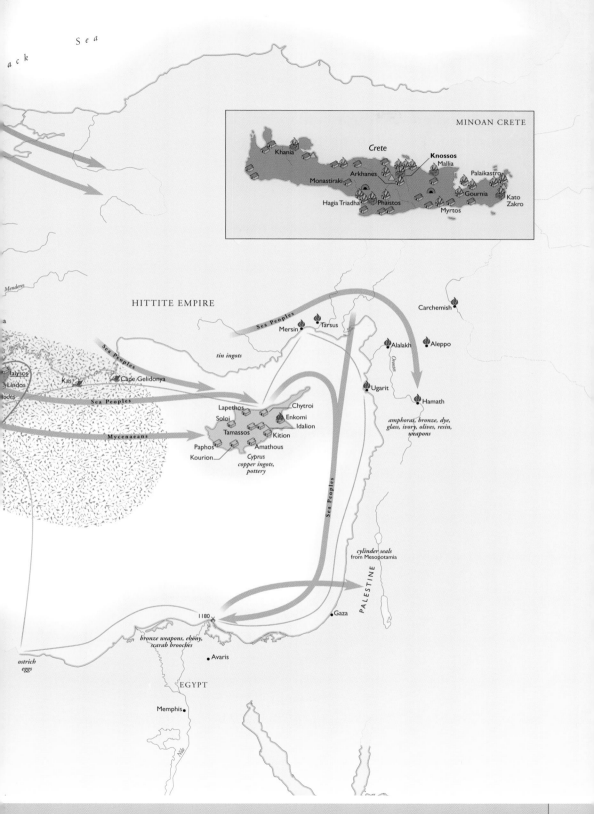

Sea

ack

Sea

MINOAN CRETE

Crete

Khania

Knossos

Mallia

Arkhanes

Monastiraki

Palaikastro

Gournia

Hagia Triadha

Phaistos

Kato
Zakro

Myrtos

Menderes

HITTITE EMPIRE

Carchemish

Sea Peoples

Mersin

Tarsus

Alalakh

Aleppo

tin ingots

Orontes

Sea Peoples

Ialysos

Lindos

Kas

Cape Gelidonya

Ugarit

Hamath

odes

Sea Peoples

Lapethos

Chytroi

*amphoras, bronze, dye,
glass, ivory, olives, resin,
weapons*

Soloi

Enkomi

Mycenaeans

Idalion

Tamassos

Kition

Paphos

Amathous

Kourion

*Cyprus
copper ingots,
pottery*

Sea Peoples

*cylinder seals
from Mesopotamia*

PALESTINE

1180

Gaza

*bronze weapons, ebony,
scarab brooches*

*ostrich
eggs*

Avaris

EGYPT

Memphis

Nile

First Civilizations in the Mediterranean

Europe's first cities and states developed on the Aegean island of Crete around 2000 BCE, where the Minoans developed a system of intensive agriculture based on wheat, olives, and vines. Olives and vines grew well on rough hillsides and produced valuable commodities for long-distance trade, allowing good plowland to be kept for wheat production.

Sheep were kept on Crete's mountain pastures and their wool supplied a textile industry that exported cloth to Egypt. Minoan pottery and metalwork were in demand throughout the eastern Mediterranean.

Minoan palace states

By 2000 BCE Minoan society was controlled from palaces at Knossos, Phaistos, Mallia, and Khania, probably the capitals of small kingdoms. The palaces were centers for redistributing produce collected as taxes or tribute for rations to support administrators, craftsmen, or traders. Around 1700 BCE most of the Minoan palaces were destroyed by fire, probably as a result, of warfare between the palace states; they were rebuilt, but only Knossos regained its former splendor. In 1626 BCE the palaces were damaged by ash falls and earthquakes resulting from a volcanic eruption on the island of Thera. The palaces were rebuilt, but the Minoan civilization collapsed in about 1450 BCE after conquest by the Mycenaeans.

Mycenaean civilization

The Mycenaeans, or Achaeans as they probably called themselves, were a Greek-speaking people who had moved to the Greek peninsula from the Balkans around 2000 BCE. By around 1600 BCE small kingdoms based on fortified towns were beginning to develop. The earliest evidence of Mycenaean civilization is a series of richly furnished shaft graves at Mycenae, dating to between

Curriculum Context

The Minoan palaces are important in understanding the characteristics of the agrarian civilizations that emerged in the second millennium BCE.

Shaft grave

A burial structure consisting of a narrow, deep shaft dug into rock.

1650 BCE and 1550 BCE. The grave goods reveal a wealthy warrior society and include hoards of bronze weapons, gold, silver, jewelry, and gold deathmasks.

A warrior society

Mycenaean towns were well defended, especially after the 14th century BCE, by strong walls, built with massive blocks of stone and bastioned gateways. Each Mycenaean stronghold was ruled over by a king with a warrior aristocracy. The kings controlled many craftsmen and hundreds of mainly female slaves. Around 1450 BCE the Mycenaeans expanded in the Aegean, conquering Crete and founding Miletos on the Anatolian coast.

The Mycenaean civilization came to a violent end around 1200 BCE. Most of the major centers were sacked and town life came to an end. The whole Aegean entered a so-called dark age which lasted about four centuries. The attackers were probably the Sea Peoples who also brought chaos to Egypt and the Levant. A power vacuum developed in Greece into which another Greek-speaking people, the Dorians, migrated around 1100 BCE, overrunning the Peloponnese, Crete, and Rhodes: of the old Mycenaean centers only Athens retained its independence.

Curriculum Context

Urban society expanded in the Aegean during the period of Mycenaean dominance. The curriculum may ask students to describe the social organization of Mycenaean towns.

Minoan and Mycenaean writing

The Minoans had a hieroglyphic script by 2000 BCE, but this was superseded by a syllabic script three centuries later. Neither script has been deciphered, so the ethnic identity of the Minoans is unknown but they did not speak an Indo-European language and were therefore not Greeks. The Mycenaeans had a system of writing, based on the Cretan syllabic script. It fell out of use when the civilization ended around 1200 BCE.

Phoenicia and Greece

The Phoenician and Greek civilizations were important trading powers in the Mediterranean in the first millennium BCE, founding colonies throughout the region.

N

ATLANTIC
OCEAN

tin

tin

tin

tin

tin

tin

Loire

Seine

Rhine

Elbe

Danube

Po

Rhône

Ebro

Douro

Tagus

Vix

Celts

Ligurians

ALPS

Spina

Etruscan
city states

Volaterrae

Volci

Gravisca

Alalia
Corsica

Kyr
Pithekous
P

Sardinia

Agathe

Massilia

Emporion

PYRENEES

Celtiberians

Iberians

Palma

Mago

Balearic
Islands

Ebusus

Hemeroskopeion

Lucentum

Tharros

Sulcis

Caralis

Nora

Himera
Soleis

Panormus

Motya

Minoa
Akraga

K

Tartessians

Huelva
(Tartessos)

Gades

Malaca

Carteia

Sexi

Mainake

Abdera

Cartenna

Rusucurru

Utica

Hippo Regius

Carthage

Tingis

Lixus

Rusaddir

Berbers

Hadrumetum

Girba

Sabrata

Oea

Leptis M

Mogador

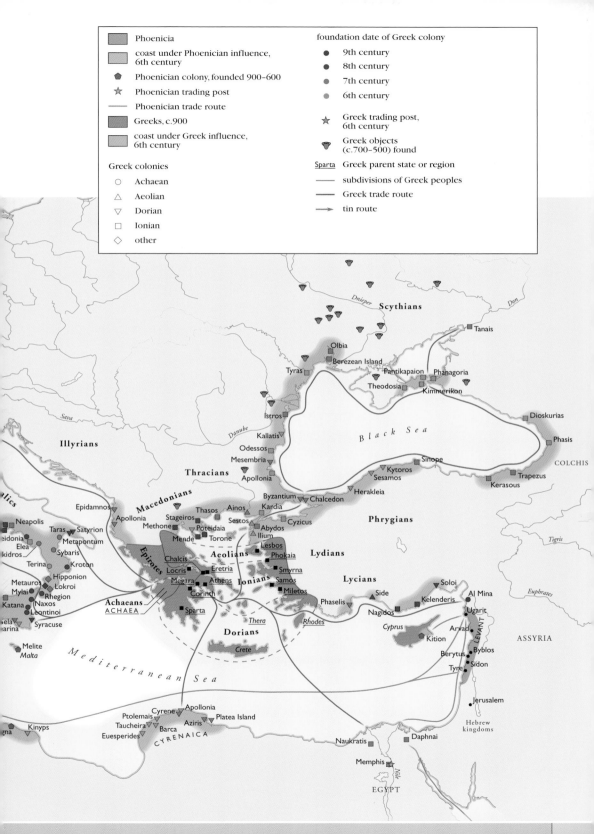

▦	Phoenicia	
▨	coast under Phoenician influence, 6th century	
⬠	Phoenician colony, founded 900–600	
★	Phoenician trading post	
—	Phoenician trade route	
▨	Greeks, c.900	
▨	coast under Greek influence, 6th century	

Greek colonies

- ○ Achaean
- △ Aeolian
- ▽ Dorian
- □ Ionian
- ◇ other

foundation date of Greek colony

- ● 9th century
- ● 8th century
- ● 7th century
- ● 6th century

- ★ Greek trading post, 6th century
- ▽ Greek objects (c.700–500) found
- Sparta Greek parent state or region
- — subdivisions of Greek peoples
- — Greek trade route
- → tin route

Scythians

Dnieper

Don

Tanais

Olbia
Berezean Island
Tyras
Pantikapaion
Phanagoria
Theodosia
Kimmerikon

Istros

Black Sea

Dioskurias
Phasis

COLCHIS

Kallatis
Odessos
Mesembria
Apollonia

Sinope
Kytoros
Sesamos
Herakleia

Trapezus
Kerasous

Illyrians

Sava

Danube

Thracians

Macedonians

Byzantium
Kardia
Chalcedon

Phrygians

Tigris

Epidamnos
Apollonia
Methone
Stageiros
Thasos
Ainos
Sestos
Abydos
Ilium
Cyzicus

Euphrates

Neapolis
...alics
Taras
Satyrion
Metapontum
...eidonia
Elea
...kidros
Sybaris
Terina
Kroton
Hipponion
Metauros
Mylai
Lokroi
Rhegion
Katana
Naxos
...gela
...arina
Leontinoi
Syracuse

Epirotes
Chalcis
Locris
Eretria
Megara
Athens
Corinth

Poteidaia
Mende
Torone

Lesbos
Phokaia
Smyrna
Samos
Miletos

Aeolians
Ionians

Lydians

Lycians

Phaselis
Side
Nagidos

Soloi
Kelenderis
Al Mina
Ugarit

Arvad

ASSYRIA

Cyprus
Kition

Achaeans
ACHAEA
Sparta

Thera
Rhodes

Dorians
Crete

Berytus
Byblos
Sidon
Tyre

Jerusalem

Melite
Malta

Mediterranean Sea

Hebrew kingdoms

Kinyps
...gna

Cyrene
Apollonia
Ptolemais
Taucheira
Barca
Aziris
Platea Island
Euesperides
CYRENAICA

Naukratis
Daphnai

Memphis

Nile

EGYPT

Phoenicia and Greece

As the eastern Mediterranean recovered from the disruptions of the late second millennium BCE, the Phoenicians and Greeks began to establish trade routes and colonies throughout the western Mediterranean and, in the case of the Greeks, the Black Sea. The first to extend their trade routes into the western Mediterranean were the Phoenicians.

N

The Phoenicians were a Levantine people culturally and linguistically related to the Canaanites. Their homeland had the best natural harbors on the coastline of the Levant, where small ports had grown up as early as the third millennium BCE. The leading Phoenician ports had developed into independent city–states by 1500 BCE, trading cedar wood, purple dye, and other commodities with Egypt.

Phoenician expansion

The earliest evidence of Phoenician expansion overseas is at Kition on Cyprus about 1000 BCE. The main period of Phoenician expansion, however, extended from the late ninth century to the mid-seventh century BCE. Phoenician colonies in Tunisia, Sicily, and Sardinia gave them control over the main approaches to the western Mediterranean. By the eighth century BCE Phoenician trade routes extended through the Straits of Gibraltar and some way along the Atlantic coasts of Spain and Morocco. By the seventh century BCE Carthage, a Tyrian colony, had become the leading Phoenician city in the west. Phoenician colonies technically remained subject to their parent cities, but they were forced to become independent when Phoenicia was conquered by the Babylonians in the sixth century BCE.

Greek recovery

For almost three centuries after the collapse of the Mycenaean civilization, Greece remained impoverished and isolated. Recovery began around 900 BCE as the Greeks reestablished trade links with the Levant and Italy. By the eighth century BCE prosperity had returned, urban life was restored, and the Greek population was rising rapidly.

Greek colonization

The earliest Greek overseas colonies, such as Al Mina in Syria and Kymai in Italy, were motivated by trade. Even before the end of the eighth century BCE, colonies had also become a way for the Greek cities to resettle surplus population. The Greek colonies, unlike Phoenician colonies, were founded from the outset to be independent states in their own right, although relations with the parent states often remained close.

The first major colonizing efforts in the eighth century BCE were in southern Italy and Sicily, where there were many good harbors and fertile agricultural land. Relations with the native peoples were poor, but that did not prevent Greek culture from having a great impact in Italy, especially on the Etruscans in the north. The Italian colonies were initially highly successful— Syracuse, for example, was the most populous Greek city in the fifth century BCE—but the constant hostility of the natives sapped their strength and by the third century BCE they were in decline.

In the seventh and sixth centuries BCE the effort of colonization shifted to the coasts of Thrace and the Black Sea. The Greek colonies here traded luxury goods with the steppe peoples for wheat to feed the cities of the Greek homeland. The same period also saw colonies founded in Cyrenaica and Egypt. The Greek colonies in Egypt became politically influential and through them the Greeks gained a deep knowledge of Egyptian art and architecture.

Greek City–States

Following the end of the dark ages, the city-state, or *polis*, became the dominant form of political organization in Greece.

N

Illyrians

Lake Prespa

MACEDO

Taras

Vijose

Mt Olym
(Z

Sybaris

PINDOS MOUNTAINS

EPIRUS

Corcyra

Dodona
(Zeus)

Pin

Corfu

THE

Ambracia

Acheloos

Ar
(A

ACARNANIA

AETOLIA

Ph
(

Kephallenia

ACHAE

ELIS

Himera

Rhegion

Zakynthos

Olympia▲
(Zeus)

ARCA
Mant

Sicily

Akragas

Gela

Syracuse

MESSEN

Mediterranea

▨	area of Greek settlement, 6th century BC
⬭	Greek territory under royal or aristocratic rulers, c.600
▨	Spartan territory, 505
▨	allies of Sparta, 505
🏛	major city-state, 6th century BC
<u>Athens</u>	tyranny at some time between 660–485
—	Persian conquests by 513
▲	site of pan-Hellenic festival
▪	Amphictonic shrine, with associated god named
▫	other major temple or shrine, with associated god named

Black Sea

Thracians

Danube

Maritsa

Herakleia

Byzantium

Chalcedon

Abdera

Thasos

Cyzicus

Strymon

Thasos

Samothrace

Imroz

Sestos

Lampsakos

Axios

Poteidaia

Lemnos

Abydos

Lesbos

SALY

Northern
Sporades

AEOLIA

Mytilene

Aegean Sea

Euboea

Chios

Phokaia

Gediz

LYDIA
conquered by Persians
547–546

Alacomenae
(Apollo)

Chalcis

Chios

Klasomenai

Kephisos

Eretria

BOEOTIA

Thebes

Kolophon

Menderes

ATTICA

Eleusis (Demeter)

Ephesos
(Artemis)

phi
llo)

Megara

Athens

Andros

Samos

Sikyon

Corinth
(Poseidon)

Ikaria

Miletos

emea
Zeus)

Argos
(Hera)

Aegina

IONIA

Didyma
(Apollo)

Tegea

Epidauros (Asclepios)
Calauria
(Poseidon)

Delos
(Apollo)

Naxos

Halikarnassos

LYCIA

parta

Paros

Naxos

Kos

Kos

LACONIA

Melos

Knidos
(Aphrodite)

KINOURIA

Thera

Ialysos

Kameiros

Rhodes

KYTHERA
(Aphrodite)

Lindos

Carpathos

Sea

Crete

Kydonia

Knossos

Itanos

Gortyn

Greek City–States

During the dark ages (1200–800 BCE), the Greeks lived in tribal communities under chiefs or kings who combined the roles of warleader and chief priest but who had to consult the warrior aristocracy. Their subjects sometimes paid tribute to the kings, but there was no regular system of taxation. Town life almost ceased in the dark ages and such long-distance trade as survived was controlled by the Phoenicians.

By the ninth century BCE power began to pass to the hereditary aristocracy, and by the end of the seventh century BCE only Sparta, Argos, and Thera still had monarchies. Little is known about the institutions of aristocratic government, but it was under aristocratic rule that trade and city life revived in Greece and that Greek colonization overseas began. The *polis* became the dominant form of political organization. The cities dominated the countryside and became the main centers of political power, commerce, and cultural life.

The Greek tyrants

In the seventh century BCE aristocratic government became unpopular. New military tactics, involving large numbers of heavily armed infantry, deprived the aristocrats of their status as a warrior elite. There was discontent also among the newly rich who, not having aristocratic birth, were excluded from political power. In many Greek city–states these discontents led, between 660 and 485 BCE, to revolutions under popular leaders known as "tyrants."

Most tyrannies endured only a few decades and were replaced with oligarchies, in which the aristocracy was influential but had no monopoly on power. Other Greek city–states reformed their constitutions without revolutions and by the sixth century BCE most were ruled by oligarchies.

Polis

A city–state in ancient Greece.

Tyrants

In ancient Greece, rulers who took power without hereditary or consititutional right.

Oligarchy

A form of goverment in which political power rests with a few elite.

From Solon to Kleisthenes

The most far-reaching political upheavals took place in Athens. Solon was appointed to reform the constitution in 594 BCE. The result was a compromise that satisfied nobody and in 546 BCE the tyrant Peisistratus seized power. Peisistratus was an effective and popular ruler who broke the aristocratic hold on power. He was succeeded by his son Hippias, who was overthrown by an aristocratic faction in 510 BCE. After three years of internal strife the aristocratic party was defeated. The reformer Kleisthenes introduced a democratic constitution which gave all 45,000 male citizens the right to attend the assembly and vote on all major decisions and appointments.

The Spartan League

By actively involving its citizens in government, Athens had become a self-confident and assertive state by 500 BCE but for most of the sixth century BCE the most powerful state was Sparta, which had taken the lead in developing new infantry tactics in which armored spearmen fought in a close-packed phalanx presenting an impenetrable hedge of spears to the enemy. Sparta formed a league of cities through which it dominated the Peloponnese.

Phalanx

A body of troops standing in close formation.

Greek cultural identity

Despite their rivalries, Greeks had a strong sense of common identity by the eighth century BCE, expressed through the name they gave themselves—Hellenes—and religion. All Greeks worshiped the same gods and celebrated pan-Hellenic festivals, such as the Olympic Games. A cultural heritage had also emerged, epitomized by the epic poems of Homer, which were composed in the eighth century BCE. The revival of trade made it necessary to re-invent writing in the eighth century BCE, as the Mycenaean script had been entirely forgotten. The Greeks adopted the Phoenician consonantal alphabet and by adding separate signs for vowels turned it into a far more flexible and simple writing system.

Etruscans, Greeks, and Carthaginians

The Etruscan civilization that emerged in the eighth century BCE became strongly influenced by Greek culture. Phoenician and Carthaginian influence extended to southern Spain.

ATLANTIC OCEAN

Seine

Loire

Mont Lass

7th-6th century BC

P Y R E N E E S

Agathe

Emporion

Ullastret

Kese

Mago

Palma

Balearic Islands

Ebusus

Elviña

Coaña

Rianxo

Cameixa

El Redal

Cortes de Navarra

Azaila

Terroso

Soldeana

Douro

C e l t i b e r i a n s

I b e r i a n s

L u s i t a n i a n s

Tagus

Saguntum

Pedra de Oiro

Guadiana

KINGDOM OF TARTESSOS
c.600

Guadalquivir

Porcuna

Hemeroskopeion

Lucentum

Elche

Elche

T u r d e t a n i a n s

T a r t e s s i a n s

Niebla

El Carambolo

Tartessos (Huelva)

Osuna

Gades

Malaca

Mainake

Sexi

Abdera

Carteia

Rusucur

Cartenna

Tingis

Lixus

Rusaddir

B e r b e r s

Etruscans, Greeks, and Carthaginians

Etruscan city–states had emerged in central Italy by 800 BCE. In the eighth century BCE cities were founded on the coasts of southern Italy, France, Spain, and north Africa by Phoenician and Greek colonists. The Greeks had a strong impact on the Etruscan civilization while the Phoenician colonies in Spain influenced the growth of cities and states among the native Tartessian and Iberian peoples by 500 BCE.

The Etruscans

The forerunner of the Etruscan civilization was the Villanova culture—the first iron-using culture in Italy—which developed in Tuscany around 900 BCE and later spread north into the Po valley. In Tuscany the Villanova culture was replaced by the Etruscan civilization in the eighth century BCE but it survived in the Po valley until the sixth century BCE, when the area was overrun by the Etruscans.

Etruria was rich in iron and copper ores, and had good agricultural land and a coastline with many natural harbors which encouraged the Etruscans to become active seafarers and traders. Most early Etruscan cities were sited a few miles from the coast. The 12 most important cities were loosely united in the Etruscan league. From the eighth century BCE the Etruscans faced competition from Greek and Phoenician colonies in the western Mediterranean. With Carthaginian help, the Etruscans succeeded in driving the Greeks out of Corsica in 535 BCE but attacks on the Greeks at Kymai (Cumae) in southern Italy were repulsed in 524, 505 and 474 BCE. Despite these hostilities, Etruscan culture had become very Hellenized by the sixth century BCE.

Latin cities

The other major group of peoples in Italy were the Italic speakers who had probably migrated into the

Curriculum Context

Students learning about the expansion of interregional trade in the first millennium BCE might be asked to focus on trade networks in the western Mediterranean.

Hellenized

Influenced by Greek culture, customs, or style.

peninsula from central Europe during Urnfield times. Although most of the Italic peoples were still organized into tribes in 500 BCE, city–states had developed among the Latins as a result of Etruscan influence. The leading Latin city was Rome. The Romans expelled their Etruscan king in 509 BCE and founded a republic but Rome was still little more than a market town.

Carthaginian and Phoenician influence

Carthage was not the earliest Phoenician colony in north Africa but its fine harbor and strategic position had made it into the most important by the mid-seventh century BCE. Although technically still subject to its parent city, Tyre, Carthage had by this time begun its own independent colonization of the Balearic Islands. In 580 BCE Carthage intervened in Sicily to protect Motya against the Greek city of Selinus and shortly after to support the Phoenician colonies in Sardinia against the natives. These actions established Carthage as the protector of the Phoenician colonies in the west and by 500 BCE it had become the capital of a loose-knit maritime empire which dominated the western Mediterranean trade routes.

The area most influenced by the Phoenicians and Carthaginians was southern Spain. Gades (Cadiz) was an important Phoenician trading post from at least the eighth century BCE, and Huelva—almost certainly the ancient city of Tartessos—was a port with trading links with the Greeks, Phoenicians, and Atlantic Europe by around 800 BCE. Huelva's prosperity was based on exports of silver and other metals from southern Spain and of tin from Galicia, Brittany, and Cornwall. By the sixth century BCE a Tartessian kingdom had developed and towns were being founded in the Guadalquivir valley. Phoenician techniques were incorporated into local metalworking and sculpture and a script based on the Phoenician alphabet was adopted.

Curriculum Context

Students may be asked to assess the Etruscan influence in the development of Roman culture.

Curriculum Context

The adoption of a Phoenician-based script in southern Spain is a good example of the cultural effects of Phoenician colonization and trade networks.

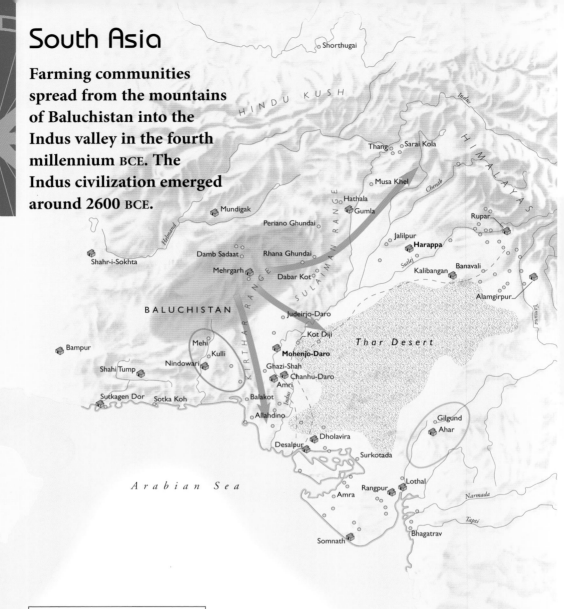

South Asia

Farming communities spread from the mountains of Baluchistan into the Indus valley in the fourth millennium BCE. The Indus civilization emerged around 2600 BCE.

N

Shorthugai

HINDU KUSH

HIMALAYAS

Indus

Thang   Sarai Kola

Musa Khel

Chenab

Hathala

Gumla

Rupar

Mundigak

Periano Ghundai

Jalilpur

Harappa

Damb Sadaat

Rhana Ghundai

Kalibangan

Banavali

Shahr-i-Sokhta

Mehrgarh

Dabar Kot

Sutlej

Helmand

SULAIMAN RANGE

KIRTHAR RANGE

Alamgirpur

Yamuna

BALUCHISTAN

Judeirjo-Daro

Kot Diji

Thar Desert

Bampur

Mehi

Kulli

Mohenjo-Daro

Shahi Tump

Nindowari

Ghazi-Shah

Chanhu-Daro

Amri

Indus

Gilgund

Ahar

Sutkagen Dor   Sotka Koh

Balakot

Allahdino

Dholavira

Desalpur

Surkotada

Arabian Sea

Rangpur

Lothal

Amra

Narmada

Tapti

Somnath

Bhagatrav

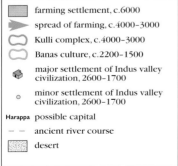

▨	farming settlement, c.6000
▶	spread of farming, c.4000–3000
◖◗	Kulli complex, c.4000–3000
◯	Banas culture, c.2200–1500
⬒	major settlement of Indus valley civilization, 2600–1700
○	minor settlement of Indus valley civilization, 2600–1700
Harappa	possible capital
– –	ancient river course
▦	desert

South Asia 600–1500

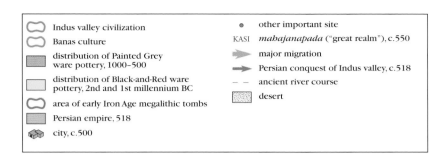

	Indus valley civilization
	Banas culture
	distribution of Painted Grey ware pottery, 1000–500
	distribution of Black-and-Red ware pottery, 2nd and 1st millennium BC
	area of early Iron Age megalithic tombs
	Persian empire, 518
	city, c.500

	other important site
KASI	*mahajanapada* ("great realm"), c.550
	major migration
	Persian conquest of Indus valley, c.518
– –	ancient river course
	desert

South Asia 1500–500 BCE

Taxila
GANDARA
Aryans from central Asia, mid 2nd millennium
KURU
Sutlej
Indus
KIRTHAR RANGE
SULAIMAN RANGE
HIMALAYAS
Thar Desert
Hastinapura
PANCHALA
Ahichhattra
KOSALA
Atranjikhera
SURASENA
Bairat
Sravasti
Lumbini
Mathura
Yamuna
Ganges
MALLA
Tilaura-kot
Kusinagara
VRIJJI
Vaisali
VATSA
Pataliputra
Campa
MATSYA
CHEDI
KASI
Rajgir
ANGA
Ahar
Kausambi
MAGADHA
AVANTI
Vidisha
Ujjain
Mahismati
Narmada
Tamluk
Arabian Sea
Tapti
Mahanadi
ASSAKA
Deccan
Bay of Bengal
Godavari
WESTERN GHATS
Krishna
EASTERN GHATS
Brahmagiri
Kaveri
Sinhalese settlement of Ceylon, c.500 BC
Ceylon
Veddas

South Asia

The first civilization of south Asia emerged in the Indus river valley around 2600 BCE. In its origins it resembled the Mesopotamian civilization: it arose on the arid floodplain of an unpredictable river where the need for large-scale irrigation and flood defense schemes led to the development of a well-organized hierarchical society.

Curriculum Context

The cities and towns of the Indus valley are a good example of the impact of trade on urban development and the emergence of social hierarchies in the third millennium BCE.

The Indus valley civilization

The first farming communities in south Asia developed at sites such as Mehrgarh in the mountains of Baluchistan as early as 6000 BCE and spread from there into the Indus valley in the fourth millennium BCE. The early farming communities of the Indus valley showed no signs of social ranking, but the transition to a hierarchical society occurred very rapidly in about 2600 BCE. This may have been a result of the establishment of trading contacts with Mesopotamia. Towns grew up in the Indus valley as a result of this trade. Metals and other products of the highlands were gathered in the towns and sent on to Mesopotamia. The growth of trade also led to the development of small towns, such as Nindowari, in the highlands.

Cities and towns

Most of the cities and towns in the Indus valley were small, but Mohenjo-Daro and Harappa (from which the Indus civilization gets its alternative name, "Harappan") had populations of around 30,000–40,000, placing them among the largest Bronze Age cities anywhere.

Both Mohenjo-Daro and Harappa had impressive mud-brick city walls, a citadel with public buildings, and granaries and streets laid out on a grid pattern. The civilization was literate, but its pictographic script has not been deciphered. As a result, the identity of the Indus people is unknown.

Decline of the Indus valley civilization

By 1800 BCE the Indus cities were in decline and a century later they had been abandoned. Writing fell out of use. To date, no entirely convincing explanation has been found for the abandonment of these cities.

Aryan migration

Sometime around 1500 BCE the Aryans, a semi-nomadic Indo-European pastoralist people, migrated into the Indian subcontinent from central Asia and occupied the northern half of the territory once covered by the Indus civilization. Some aspects of Indus culture were absorbed by the Aryans and the pottery styles of the late Indus Banas culture survived, but all memory of the civilization itself was lost; it was rediscovered only in the 1920s.

Around 1100 BCE the Aryans adopted iron working and soon afterward they moved east and began to settle down in villages on the Ganges plain as rice farmers. The appearance, around 1000–800 BCE, across the Ganges plain, of the Painted Gray ware pottery style has been linked to the Aryan settlement of the area.

The Gangetic civilization

By 900 BCE small tribal kingdoms and aristocratic tribal republics, known collectively as *janapadas*, were developing across the Ganges plain. By 700 BCE they had coalesced to form 16 *mahajanapadas* ("great realms"). By 500 BCE Magadha had emerged as the most powerful. Hand in hand with the process of state formation went the growth of cities. This was the formative period of the Hindu religion and the late sixth century witnessed the lives and teachings of Mahavira, the founder of Jainism, and of Siddhartha Gautama, the Buddha. By 500 BCE the Gangetic civilization extended as far south as the River Godavari.

Pastoralist people

People who live an agricultural lifestyle based on the raising and herding of livestock such as sheep or cattle.

Curriculum Context

In a study of cultural patterns in northern India in the second millennium BCE, the curriculum may require students to assess the impact of the Aryan migration on the peoples of northern India.

East Asia

Civilization first emerged in east Asia in the second millennium BCE. China's first great dynasty was the Shang. In the Zhou dynasty society was organized on a feudal system.

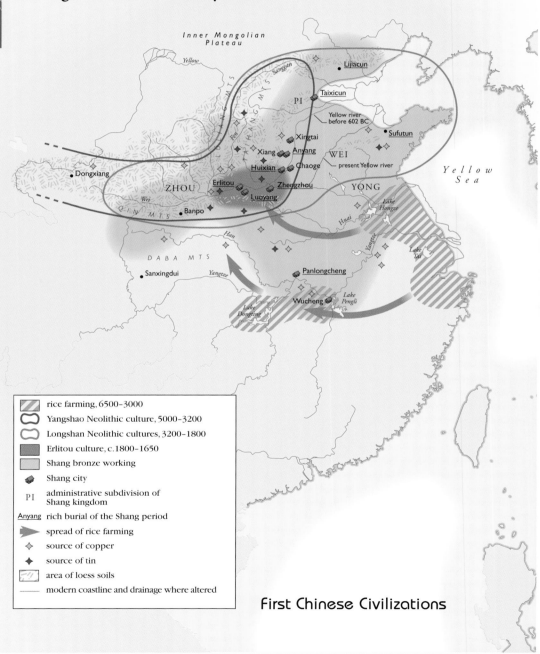

Inner Mongolian Plateau

Yellow

Lijiacun

Taixicun

PI

Yellow river before 602 BC

Xingtai

Xiang

Anyang

Sufutun

WEI

Huixian

Chaoge

present Yellow river

Dongxiang

ZHOU

Erlitou

Zhengzhou

YONG

Banpo

Luoyang

Lake Hongze

Wei

Han

Huai

Yangtze

Lake Tai

DABA MTS

Sanxingdui

Yangtze

Panlongcheng

Lake Pengli

Wucheng

Lake Dongting

Yellow Sea

First Chinese Civilizations

▨	rice farming, 6500–3000
⌇	Yangshao Neolithic culture, 5000–3200
⌇	Longshan Neolithic cultures, 3200–1800
▰	Erlitou culture, c.1800–1650
▱	Shang bronze working
⬢	Shang city
PI	administrative subdivision of Shang kingdom
Anyang	rich burial of the Shang period
➤	spread of rice farming
✧	source of copper
✦	source of tin
▱	area of loess soils
—	modern coastline and drainage where altered

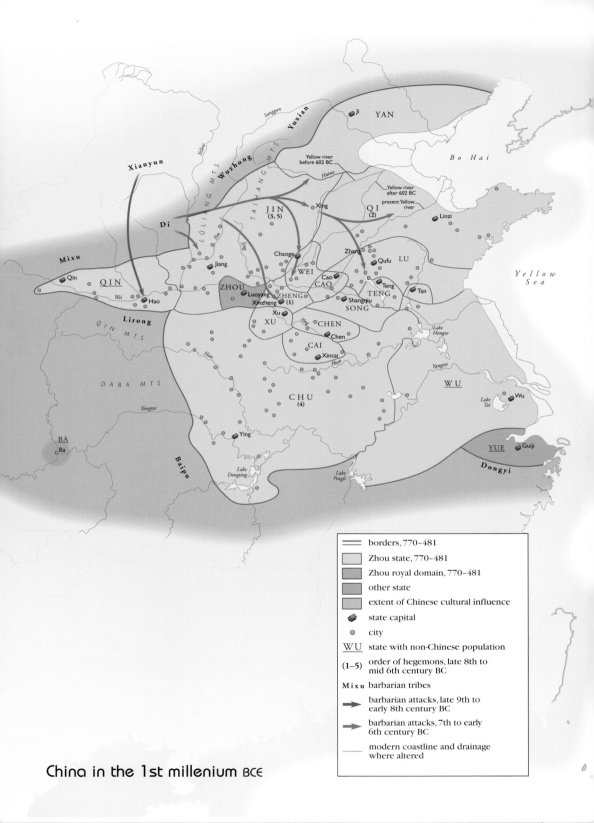

China in the 1st millenium BCE

Legend:

- borders, 770–481
- Zhou state, 770–481
- Zhou royal domain, 770–481
- other state
- extent of Chinese cultural influence
- state capital
- city
- WU — state with non-Chinese population
- (1–5) — order of hegemons, late 8th to mid 6th century BC
- Mixu — barbarian tribes
- barbarian attacks, late 9th to early 8th century BC
- barbarian attacks, 7th to early 6th century BC
- modern coastline and drainage where altered

Map labels:

Xianyun, Di, Mixu, Qin, QIN, Wei, Hao, Lirong, QIN MTS, DABA MTS, Yangtze, BA, Ba, Baipu, Lake Dongting, Han, Ying, Jiang, Fen, Jing, JIN (3, 5), Chaoge, ZHOU, Luoyang, Xinzheng, ZHENG (1), Xu, XU, WEI, Cao, CAO, Zhang, Qufu, LU, Teng, TENG, Tan, Shangqiu, SONG, CHEN, Chen, CAI, Xincai, Huai, CHU (4), Lake Hongse, Yangtze, Lake Tai, WU, Wu, Lake Pengli, YUE, Guiji, Dongyi, Yellow Sea, Bo Hai, Ji, YAN, Sanggan, Yellow, LÜLIANG MTS, Wuzhong, Yuxian, TAIHANG MTS, Hutuo, Xing, QI (2), Linzi, Yellow river before 602 BC, Yellow river after 602 BC, present Yellow river

East Asia

The first civilization of east Asia developed in the Yellow River valley in the 18th century BCE from indigenous Neolithic cultures. Farming began as early as 5800 BCE on the broad band of loess soils that stretches across the Yellow River basin. By 5000 BCE millet farming villages of the Yangshao culture were spread across much of the region.

At the same time rice farming communities were spreading among the wetlands of the Yangtze valley. Rice farming spread to the Yellow River valley in the late fourth millennium BCE. The population rose, copper came into use, regional trading networks developed, and a warrior class emerged. There is evidence of warfare, such as rammed earth fortifications and massacres of prisoners. A system of divination based on the use of oracle bones was developed.

According to Chinese traditions, civilization was founded by the emperor Huang Di around 2698 BCE while the first dynasty, the Xia, was founded by Yu the Great in about 2205 BCE. However, there is no evidence for states in China in the third millennium BCE.

The Shang dynasty

The first historically and archeologically attested Chinese dynasty is the Shang. This was founded about 1766 BCE by King Tang. Cities with monumental buildings began to develop craft specialization and advanced bronze-casting techniques were adopted. The appearance of rich burials points to the emergence of a powerful ruling elite. A pictographic script came into use: the modern Chinese script is its direct descendant. Shang cultural influence extended across most of northern China and as far south as the Yangtze river. Like many early states, the Shang kingdom combined directly run provinces and vassal states.

The Zhou dynasty

Around 1122 BCE the Shang king Di-xin was defeated and overthrown by his vassal king Wu of Zhou. The dynasty established by Wu became the longest lived of Chinese history and the early centuries of its rule were looked back on as a golden age. To legitimize their rule, the Zhou rulers introduced the theory of the "Mandate of Heaven." The ruler was the "Son of Heaven" and "All under Heaven" was his lawful domain so long as he was just and moral. Should a ruler become unjust, Heaven would send him a warning; if he failed to reform, the Mandate would be given to another. Di-xin had been a sadist, so Heaven had transferred the right to rule to the Zhou. This theory, which could be used both to condemn disobedience to the ruler and to justify successful usurpation, remained central to Chinese imperial ideology.

The Zhou kingdom was a decentralized feudal state, divided into fiefs governed by dukes chosen from among the king's relatives and trusted supporters. Only the royal domain was directly ruled by the king.

The Springs and Autumns period

In 770 BCE barbarian attacks on Hao forced the Zhou to move their capital to Luoyang. This event marks the beginning of the period of disorder and fragmentation known as the Springs and Autumns period (after the title of the annals of the state of Lu).

The Springs and Autumns period was a brutal age but it saw great creativity in literature and religious and philosophical thought. The end of the period saw Confucius found the ethical system that bears his name. The Springs and Autumns period turned into the Warring States period (480–221 BCE), which saw the decline of feudal relationships and the rise of a professional bureaucracy.

Confucius

An ancient Chinese philosopher. Confucius became the most influential philosopher in ancient China and his ethical system remains fundamental to Chinese thought.

The Americas

The first civilization in Mesoamerica was the Olmec from around 1200 BCE. The earliest complex societies to develop in South America emerged on the desert coast of Peru.

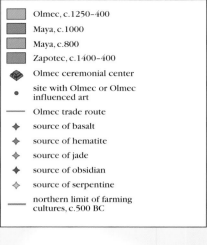

	Olmec, c.1250–400
	Maya, c.1000
	Maya, c.800
	Zapotec, c.1400–400
⬢	Olmec ceremonial center
•	site with Olmec or Olmec influenced art
—	Olmec trade route
✦	source of basalt
✦	source of hematite
✦	source of jade
✦	source of obsidian
✧	source of serpentine
—	northern limit of farming cultures, c.500 BC

Pavón

Capacha

El Opeño

Tlatilco
Valley of Mexico
Cuicuilco • Tlapacoya
Gualupita
Chalcatzinco • Los Bocas
Balsas

El Trapiche
El Viejón

Gulf of Mexico

Komchen
Dzibilchaltun

Oxtotitlan • Tehuacán Valley
Juxtiahuaca

Tres Zapotes

Yucatán Peninsula

Monte Negro
Oaxaca Valley
Monte Albán

San José Mogote
Las Limas
Dainzú

Laguna de los Cerros
La Venta
San Lorenzo

Balancán

Nakbe

Cuello
Lamanai
Uaxactún

Tikal

Padre Piedra
Pijijiapan • Xoc

Altar de Sacríficios

Salinas la Blanca • Izapa
Abaj Takalik

Copán
Kaminaljuyú

Chalchuapa

PACIFIC OCEAN

Civilizations of Mesoamerica

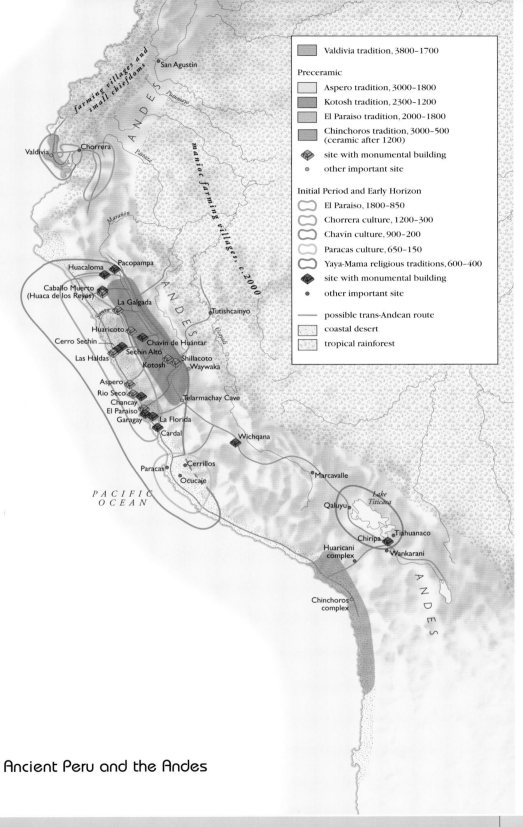

Valdivia tradition, 3800–1700

Preceramic
- Aspero tradition, 3000–1800
- Kotosh tradition, 2300–1200
- El Paraiso tradition, 2000–1800
- Chinchoros tradition, 3000–500 (ceramic after 1200)
- site with monumental building
- other important site

Initial Period and Early Horizon
- El Paraiso, 1800–850
- Chorrera culture, 1200–300
- Chavín culture, 900–200
- Paracas culture, 650–150
- Yaya-Mama religious traditions, 600–400
- site with monumental building
- other important site
- possible trans-Andean route
- coastal desert
- tropical rainforest

San Agustin

farming villages and small chiefdoms

ANDES

Putumayo

Valdivia

Chorrera

Parana

manioc farming villages, c. 2000

Marañón

ANDES

Pacopampa

Huacaloma

Caballo Muerto (Huaca de los Reyes)

La Galgada

Tutishcainyo

Ucayali

Huaricoto

Cerro Sechín

Chavín de Huántar

Las Haldas

Sechín Alto

Kotosh

Shillacoto

Waywaka

Aspero

Rio Seco

Chancay

Telarmachay Cave

El Paraiso

Garagay

La Florida

Cardal

Wichqana

Paracas

Cerrillos

Ocucaje

Marcavalle

PACIFIC OCEAN

Lake Titicaca

Qaluyu

Chiripa

Tiahuanaco

Huaricani complex

Wankarani

ANDES

Chinchoros complex

Ancient Peru and the Andes

The Americas

The domestication of maize (corn) around 2700 BCE made possible the development of permanent farming villages in Mesoamerica by 2300 BCE. Most early farmers practiced slash-and-burn agriculture, which cannot support dense populations. The Olmec became the first Mesoamerican civilization, flourishing in southeastern Mexico from around 1200 BCE to around 400 BCE.

Curriculum Context

Maize cultivation is key to understanding the development of complex societies in Mesoamerica.

Curriculum Context

The curriculum may require students to evaluate the achievements of the Olmec civilization. Olmec monumental stone sculptures are considered among the most important ancient American artworks.

On fertile river floodplains in the tropical forests of southeastern Mexico, reliable rainfall and year-round warmth made it possible to raise four crops of maize a year, which provided the economic base of the Olmec civilization.

The Olmec civilization

By 1250 BCE the Olmec lived in chiefdoms or small states ruled by a powerful hereditary elite. The most important sites were ceremonial centers with earth pyramid mounds and monumental stone sculptures. Associated with the centers were settlements of two to three thousand people. The ritual centers were periodically destroyed and sculptures defaced or buried. It is possible that this was due to warfare between states, but it is more likely that it served a ritual purpose, marking the end of calendrical cycles, the death of a ruler, or the accession of a new dynasty.

Trade and gift exchange

Trade and gift exchange played an important part in the Olmec way of life. The Olmec lands have few natural resources and the raw materials for everyday tools, so stone sculpture and status-enhancing display objects had to be imported over long distances. Gift exchange played an important part in the diffusion of Olmec culture as the emerging elites of neighboring communities took up Olmec beliefs and artifacts.

Carved in rare blue jade, this tiny bust of a woman has the distinctive monumental quality which characterizes all Olmec sculpture.

Hieroglyphic script and calendar

Late in their history, the Olmec developed a rudimentary hieroglyphic script which was used mainly for astronomical inscriptions. They used—and may have originated—both the Mesoamerican 260-day sacred year and the 52-year "long-count" calendar.

The Maya

The Maya originated about 1200 BCE in the Guatemalan highlands, developing from earlier archaic cultures, and began to spread out into the lowlands of the Yucatán peninsula around 1000 BCE. By draining and canalizing swamps the Maya were able to produce sufficient food to support a complex society and by 600 BCE towns with monumental temple pyramids, such as Nakbe and Komchen, were developing.

The Oaxaca valley civilization

Complex societies also developed among the Zapotec people of the Oaxaca valley by the first millennium BCE. Here food production was increased by simple irrigation techniques and terracing. By 400 BCE there

Curriculum Context

The Olmec hieroglyphic script and calendar are examples of major Olmec contributions to Mesoamerican civilization.

were at least seven small states in the valley, the most important of which was centered on Monte Albán, and a system of hieroglyphic writing had been developed. In the Valley of Mexico highly productive agriculture using *chinampas* led to the development of trading networks, a market economy, craft specialization, and large villages by around 200 BCE.

Complex societies in South America

The earliest complex societies in South America developed on the desert coast of Peru in settled fishing communities during the Preceramic period (3750–1800 BCE). The marine resources of this area are unusually rich and these communities were able to free labor for the construction of temples and ceremonial centers under the direction of village leaders. One of the earliest such centers was built at Aspero around 2600 BCE: it consisted of six mounds topped with masonry ceremonial structures. Cotton, squash, and gourds (used as floats for fishing nets) were cultivated, but farming did not make a significant contribution to the diet. In the highlands, herding alpacas or llamas and cultivation of root crops such as potatoes, ullucu, and oca or quinua, a cereal, gradually replaced hunting and gathering during the Preceramic period; permanent villages also developed.

The Initial Period

During the Initial Period (1800–800 BCE) the area of cultivable land in the coastal lowlands was greatly extended through irrigation works, diverting water from the rivers which flowed from the Andes through the desert to the coast. Pottery was adopted. Huge U-shaped ceremonial centers were constructed, requiring the control of considerable resources of labor, food supplies, and raw materials: one at Garagay is estimated to have required 3.2 million work-days to complete. These sites were probably focal points for local chiefdoms, but burial practices show few distinctions of wealth or rank. Interaction between the fishing communities on the coast and the farming communities in the desert river valleys and the mountains was considerable, with salt, seaweed, and dried fish from the coast being exchanged for foods such as root crops and grain from the highlands and river valleys.

The Early Horizon

The Early Horizon (about 800–200 BCE) saw the development of sophisticated architecture and complex sculptural styles at the highland ceremonial center of Chavín de Huántar. The Chavín style was the culmination of styles which had originated as early as 1200 BCE in other Andean and coastal sites. Chavín had a population of two to three thousand at its peak in the fourth century BCE but thereafter it declined without developing into a full urban civilization. Complex societies, united by common beliefs, also developed in the Lake Titicaca basin during the Early Horizon. Particularly important is the ceremonial center at Chiripa, built 600–400 BCE, in which can be seen the origins of the architectural styles of the fifth-century CE Tiahuanaco state. Maize became an important crop in the Andes during this period.

Fanged gods with human-animal attributes rendered in complex geometry are found in the widespread Chavín style, seen here on a textile design.

Glossary

Akhenaten The Egyptian pharaoh first known as Amenophis IV. Akhenaten tried to replace Egypt's traditional polytheism with the monotheistic cult of the Aten or sun disk.

Barrow An ancient burial mound consisting of a large mound of earth or stones placed over a burial site.

Chinampas An ancient Mesoamerican method of agriculture in which raised fields are built on reclaimed swamps.

City–state An independent country consisting of a city and its surrounding territory.

Confucius An ancient Chinese philosopher. Confucius became the most influential philosopher in China and his ethical system remains fundamental to Chinese thought.

Divination Telling the future by connecting with divine spirits.

Dry farming zone An arid area of the Mesopotamian plain, where it is possible to grow drought-resistant crops without the use of irrigation.

Dynasty A succession of rulers from the same family or line.

Fertile Crescent The region extending from the foothills of Iraq's Zagros mountains through south Turkey, to western Syria, Lebanon, and Israel.

Grave goods Objects left with the body of a dead person at the time of burial or cremation. Examples included the personal possessions of the deceasedd, textiles, weapons, pottery, and jewelry.

Hellenized Influenced by Greek culture, customs, or style.

Homo erectus An extinct species of humans that lived from about 1.8 million years ago.

Hunter–gatherers People who obtain most of their food by hunting wild animals and eating plants, nuts, and berries gathered from the wild.

Levant The part of the Fertile Crescent that borders the Mediterranean Sea.

Mesopotamia "The Land Between the Rivers" lay between the Tigris and Euphrates rivers, in part of what is now Iraq. The area was home to several early civilizations.

Middle Assyrian period The period of Assyrian expansion after Assyria regained its independence from Mitanni, around 1400 BCE. The period ended in 1076 BCE.

Neanderthal An extinct humanlike species that lived between about 150,000 and 35,000 years ago.

Old Kingdom The period of Egyptian history (*c.*2575–2134 BCE) when Egypt achieved its first high point of civilization. The Old Kingdom is sometimes referred to as "the Age of the Pyramids."

Oligarchy A form of government in which political power rests with a few elite.

Oracle bones Inscribed animal bones or shells used for telling the future.

Pastoralist people People who live an agricultural lifestyle based on the raising and herding of livestock such as sheep or cattle.

Phalanx A body of troops standing in close formation.

Polis A city–state in ancient Greece.

Preceramic A term used to describe a period of society prior to the use of ceramics or pottery.

Satrap A governor of a province in ancient Persia.

Sea Peoples A group of seafaring people who invaded Egypt around 1200 BCE. They may have come from the islands of the Aegean.

Semi-sedentary A semi-sedentary way of life involves living in a settled community for part of the year, usually when food is plentiful, and being nomadic for the remainder of the time.

Shaft grave A burial structure consisting of a narrow, deep shaft dug into rock.

Tyrants In ancient Greece, rulers who took power without hereditary or constitutional right.

Vassal state A state that is controlled by another more powerful state. Vassal states usually had to pay a tribute to the dominant state and provide military assistance when required.

Vizier A high-ranking political official or advisor.

Ziggurat A high Mesopotamian temple tower in the form of a stepped or terraced pyramid. Ziggurats were Mesopotamia's most distinctive monuments.

Further Research

BOOKS

Allan, Tony. *Ancient China: Cultural Atlas for Young People*. Chelsea House Publications, 2007.

Bellwood, Peter. *First Farmers: The Origins of Agricultural Societies*. Wiley-Blackwell, 2004.

Burstein, Stanley M., and Richard Shek. *Holt World History: Ancient Civilizations*. Holt McDougal, 2006.

Crompton, Samuel Willard. *Cyrus the Great*, "Ancient World Leaders" series. Chelsea House Publications, 2008.

Grguric, Nicolas. *The Mycenaeans c.1650–1100 BC*. Osprey Publishing, 2005.

Hunter, Erica C. D., and Mike Corbishley. *First Civilizations: Cultural Atlas for Young People*. Facts on File, revised edition, June 2003.

Marston, Elsa. *The Phoenicians*, "Cultures of the Past" series. Benchmark Books, 2001.

Nardo, Don. *Ancient Egypt*. Lucent Books, 2006.

Nardo, Don. *Peoples and Empires of Ancient Mesopotamia*. Lucent Books, 2008.

Nardo, Don. *The Etruscans*. Lucent Books, 2004.

Nardo, Don. *The Minoans*. Lucent Books, 2004.

Roberts, J. M. *Prehistory and the First Civilizations* (The Illustrated History of the World, Volume 1). Oxford University Press, USA, 2002.

Schomp, Virginia. *Ancient Mesopotamia: The Sumerians, Babylonians, and Assyrians*. Childrens Press, 2005.

Schomp, Virgnia. *The Ancient Chinese*. Childrens Press, 2005.

Tarling, Nicholas (ed). *The Cambridge History of Southeast Asia*. Cambridge University Press, 2000.

Tattersall, Ian. *The World from Beginnings to 4000 BCE*, "The New Oxford World History" series. Oxford University Press, 2008.

Wood, Michael. *In Search of the First Civilizations*. BBC Books, 2007.

INTERNET RESOURCES

Ancient and Lost Civilizations. A site with information about ancient civilizations throughout the world, including the Olmec and Maya civilizations of Mesoamerica. www.crystalinks.com/ancient.html

Ancient Civilizations. A British Museum website providing information on ancient civilizations arranged by theme, including cities, writing, and technology. There are also links to other British Museum websites, with information on ancient China, early imperial China, ancient India, ancient Egypt, and Mesopotamia. www.ancientcivilizations.co.uk/home_set.html

History of the World. A comprehensive list of 400 accessible articles on world history, including information relating to early farmers and the first civilizations. The articles are listed alphabetically, so it is easy to find the information you want. www.historyworld.net/wrldhis/listhistories1.asp

Human Origins. A Natural History Museum website with information about how modern humans evolved. www.nhm.ac.uk/nature-online/life/human-origins/index.html

TimeMaps: **Timeline of Ancient World History**. A website offering maps and a timeline of ancient world history, which can be navigated chronologically or geographically. The site shows the development of different civilizations, empires, and nations, beginning at the origins of civilizations in Mesopotamia in 3500 BCE. www.worldhistory.timemaps.com/ancient-world/1000BC.htm

World Civilizations. A site from Washington State University offering comprehensive background information on the world's first civilizations, including the Mesopotamian, Minoan, Mycenaean, and Chinese civilizations. www.wsu.edu/~dee/

Index

Page numbers in *italic* refer to illustrations.

Achemenes 56
Achemenid Persian empire 54–57
Adad-nirari II 47
Africa, origin of humans 14, 15
agriculture
    animal husbandry 66
    Bronze-Age Europe 74
    cereal crops 18, 19, 22, 23, 66,
        98, 102, 105
    China 98
    chinampas 104
    domestication of animals 18,
        19, 22, 23, 66
    domestication of plants 18, 19,
        20, 22, 23, 66, 102
    east Asia 98
    Europe 64, 66–67
    farming economies 18, 19, 20,
        22, 23, 102
    Fertile Crescent 18–19, 20, 22
    horses 74
    Indus valley 94
    intensive 28, 74, 78
    irrigation 26, 28, 94, 103
    Mesopotamian plain 26–27, 28
    Neolithic Europe 64, 66
    plow technology 28, 74
    rice 18, 98
    rise of 16–19, 20–23, 24–27,
        64–67
    selective breeding 18, 22
    South America 104
Ahab 53
Akhenaten 40, 41, 62
Akkad civilization 33, 34, 36, 37
Al Mina 83
alphabet
    Aramaic 46, 57
    Phoenician 87, 91
    see also writing
Amenemhet I 60
Amenophis IV *see* Akhenaten
Americas 100–105
    early humans 15
    Peleoindians 15
Amorite dynasties 36–37
Anatolia 23, 26, *27*, 36, 37, 40, 42,
    46
Andes region
    Early Horizon 105
    Initial Period 104–105
    Preceramic period 104
Aramaeans 42, 43, 46
Aramaic 46, 57
Armenia 37, 48
Aryans 8, 95

Ashur 43, 46, 47
Ashur-uballit I 42
Ashurbanipal 48, *48*, 49
Ashurnasirpal II 47
Aspero 104
Assyrian empire 36, 37, 41,
    42–43, 44, 46–49, *48*, 53
    administration of empire 47–48
    mail system 47, 57
Astyages 56
Aten, cult of the 62
Athens
    democracy 87
    reforms of Kleisthenes 87
    reforms of Solon 87
    war with Persians 57

Babylon 36, 37, 40, 42, 43, 47, 48,
    56
Babylonian empire 44, 49, 53
Balearic islands 91
Baluchistan 92, 94
Bandkeramik culture 66–67
barrows 73, 75
Bell Beaker culture *68*, 69
Bible 52
Bible Lands 50–53
bricks 43
    mud 23, 26, 94
Bronze Age
    burial practices 73, 74, 75
    China 98
    Egypt 61
    Europe 70–75
    Indus valley 94
    militarization 75
    population increase 73
    settlements 73
    Sumerian civilization 33
    Urnfield culture 74–75
    weaponry 33, 73, 75
burial practices
    Andes region 104–105
    Bronze Age 73, 74, 75
    China 98
    Neolithic 67–68, 69
    Sumerian civilization 33
    Urnfield culture 74–75

calendar 102, 103
Cambyses 56
Canaan 41, 42, 52
Carchemish, battle of 49, 53
Carthage 82, 88, 90, 91
cereals
    domestication of 18, 19, 20,
        22, 23
    Europe 66
    South America 104
    see also agriculture

Chaldeans 43, 46, 48
chariots 41, 61, *62*
Chatal Huyuk 26, *27*
Chavín de Huántar 105, *105*
Chayonu 23
chiefdoms
    Egypt 60
    Europe 69, 72
    Middle East 27
    Olmec 102
China
    Confucius 99
    Shang dynasty 96, 98
    Zhou dynasty 96, 99
cities, Mesopotamian 30–33
city–states 30, 32, 33, 36, 46, 82
    Etruscan 88, 90
    Greek 84–87
    Latin 91
clay stamps *27*
clay tablets 57
climate change 15, 18, 22, 73
colonies
    Greek 90
    Italian 83
    Phoenician 82, 90
Confucius 99
copper 19, 90
    Europe 69, 72
    smelting 26, 27
Cord Impressed Ware culture 69
Corsica 90
Crete 76, 78
Croesus, king of Lydia 56
cuneiform 57
Cyprus 82
Cyrenaica 83
Cyrus the Great 49, 53, 54, 56

Damascus 41
Darius 56, 57
dark age 79, 86
David (king of Jews) 52
democracy, Athenian 87
Di-xin 99
Diaspora 53
divination 98
Dorians 79

Eannatum of Lagash 33
Egypt 42, 53, 58–63
    conflict with Hittites 41
    control of Levant 40, 41, 49,
        60, 61
    cultural influence on Greece 83
    Middle Kingdom 58, 60
    New Kingdom 61–63
    Old Kingdom 60
    part of Persian empire 56, 63
    use of bronze 61

einkorn 22, 27, 66
Elam 36, 43, 48
emmer wheat 22, 23, 27, 66
empires, first 34–37
Eridu 28
Esarhaddon 48
Eshnunna 37
Etruscan civilization 83, 88, 90
Europe
    development of agriculture
      64–67
    Bronze Age 70–75
    Neolithic period 64–69

farming *see* agriculture
Fertile Crescent 18–19, 20, 22
flax 23
fossils 14, 15

Gangetic civilization 95
Gaza 63
glass 43
grave goods 67, 68, *68*, 69
    Bronze Age 73, 75
    Mycenaean 78, 79
Greece 80, 84–87, 88, 90
    city–states 84–87
    colonies 83
    dark age 79, 82–83, 86
    early farming settlements 64
Gutians 36

Halafian culture 27–28, 29
Hamadan 57
Hammurabi 37
Hanging Gardens of Babylon 49
Harappa 94
Hassuna culture 26–27
Hebrew kingdoms 50–53
Hebrews 42, 48, 53
henges 69
Hezekiah 53
hierarchical societies 19, 29, 47,
    64, 69
    China 98
    Indus valley 94
    see also burial practices
hieroglyphics 79, 103, 104
Hindu religion 95
Hippias 87
Hittites 37, 38–42, 41, *41*, 46, 62,
    63
Homer 87
Homo erectus 14
Homo sapiens 12, 14
Hoshea (king of Israel) 53
Huang Di 98
humans, origin of 14
hunter–gatherers 15, 16, 18, 19,
    22, 23, 66

Hurrians 37, 40, 42
Hyksos 60, 61, *62*

Ice Age 14, 15, 18
Indus 57
Indus valley civilization 92–95
Ionian Greeks 56, 57
Iran 46
iron 19, 90
    Iron Age 43, 72
    smelting 43
    tools 75
irrigation 26, 28, 94, 103
Israel 47, 52, 53
Italy, colonies 83

Jehu 53
Jericho proto-Neolithic site 23
Jerusalem 49, 52, 53
Jewish monarchy 52–53
Josiah 53
Judah 47, 48, 49, 52, 53

Kalhu 47
Kaskas 42
Kassite kingdom 37, 42, 43
Kish 33, 36
Kition, Cyprus 82
Kleisthenes 87
Knossos 78
Kush, kingdom of 61, 63
Kymai 83

Lake Titicaca 105
law code 33
Levant 22, 38, 40, 47, 49, 53, 60
    Aramaeans 46
    Assyrian power 47, 53
    coalition of states 47
    control by Egypt 40, 41, 60, 61
    farming settlements 22, 26
Libya 56
Linear Pottery culture 66–67
Lugalzagesi 33, 36
Luoyang 99
Lydia 56

mail system
    Assyrian empire 47
    Persian empire 57
maize 18, 19, 102, 105
Mandate of Heaven 99
Marathon, battle of 57
Maya 10, 103
Medes 46, 49, 56
Mediterranean, first civilizations
    76–79
megaliths
    stone circles 69
    tombs 68, 73

Mehrgarh 94
Mentuhotpe 60
Mesilim of Kish 33
Mesoamerica 100–104
    farming 19
Mesopotamia 24, 36, 40, 46
    advanced farmers 26–27
    cities 30–33
    civilization decline of 49
    empires 34–37
    Halafian culture 27–28, 29
    Hassuna culture 26–27
    Samarran culture 28
    Sumerian civilization 28, 30,
      32–33, 36, 37
    Ubaid culture 28–29
    Uruk period 30, 32, 36
    see also Assyrian empire;
    Babylonian empire
metalworking 91
    China 98
    Europe 69, 72–73
    Hittite *41*
    Middle East 26
    Minoan 78
    Phoenician techniques 91
    smelting and casting 19, 26,
      43, 69
    see also weaponry
Mexico 102
Middle East farmers 20–29
migrations 37, 42, 63, 66
    Aryans 95
    Sea Peoples 42, 63, 79
Miletos 79
Minoan civilization 76, 78
Mittani kingdom 38, 40, 41, 42
Mohenjo-Daro 94
monotheism 62
mounds, Aspero 104
mud bricks 23, 26, 94
Mursilis 37
Muwatalllis II 41
Mycenean civilization 76, 78–79

Nabonidus 49
Nabopolassar 49
Natufians 22
Neanderthals 14, 15
Nebuchadnezzar 44, 49, 53
Necho II 49
Neolithic period 22, 26
    Europe 64–67
Nindowari 94
Nineveh 42, 43, 46, 48, 49
Nubia 60, 61, 62, 63

Oaxaca valley 103–104
obsidian 23, 26, 27
Old Testament 53

oligarchy, Greek 86
Olmec civilization 100, 102–103, *103*
Olympic Games 87
Omri 53
oracle bones 98
Orkney Islands 67

Paleoindians 15
parchment 57
Pasargadae 56, 57
Peisistratus 87
Peloponnese 87
Persepolis 57
Persian empire 49, 54–57
Peru 101, 104
phalanx 87
pharaohs Egyptian 63
Philistines 42, 52
Phoenicia 80, 82, 86, 90, 91
Phrygians 42, 46
Plataea, battle of 57
plow technology 28, 74
polis 84–87
pottery
    Andes region 104
    Aryan 95
    early farming settlements 19
    glazed 43
    Hassuna culture 27
    kilns 19, 27
    Middle East 23, 24, 26, 27
    Minoan 78
    Ubaid culture 29
pyramids 60

Ramesses II 38, 41, 63
Rehoboam 52
religion
    Egyptian 62
    Eridu 28, 29
    Hindu 95
rice 18, 95, 98
Rome 91

Sakas 56
Salamis, battle of 57
Samaria 53
Samarran culture 28
Sardinia 82, 91
Sargon II 48
Sargon of Agade 34, 36
satraps 57
Saul 52
sculpture
    Andean 105
    Olmec 102, 103
Scythians 57
Sea Peoples 42, 63, 79

Sennacherib 48
Senwosret III 60
Seqenenre II 61
shaft graves 78
Shalmaneser III 47
Shamshi-Adad 36, 37
Shang dynasty 96, 98
Sicily 82, 83
Siddhartha Gautama 95
slavery 33, 79
Smerdis 56
Solomon 52
Solon 87
South America 101, 104–105
South Asia 92–95
Sparta 86
Spartan League 87
spinning 19
Springs and Autumns period 99
steppes 15, 18, 67, 83
stone circles 69
Sumerian civilization 28, 30, 32–33, 36, 37
Suppiluliumas 40
Susa 57
Syracuse 83
Syria 83

temples 28–29, 32, 33, 63
Thebes 58
Third Dynasty of Ur 36
Thrace 57, 83
Tiglath-pileser I 42, 43
Tiglath-pileser III 47, 53
tin 72, 91
tools
    agricultural 19
    axes 19, 66
    bronze 43, 73
    copper 69
    iron 43, 75
    obsidian 23, 26, 27
    stone 19, 23, 26, 29, 67, 69, 73
trade
    Greek 80, 82, 83, 86, 87
    Indus valley 94
    long-distance 23, 26, 70, 72, 78, 86
    Mediterranean 78, 82, 90, 91
    obsidian 23, 26
    Olmec 102
    Phoenician 80, 82, 86
    Sumerian 32–33
    tin 72, 91
    Ubaid culture 29
tribute 37, 47, 53, 56, 57, 78, 86
Tukulti-Ninurta I 42
Tutankhamun *62*
Tuthmosis I 40, 61

Tuthmosis IV 40
tyrants, Greek 86

Ubaid culture 28–29
Unetice culture 72
Ur-Nammu 36
Urartu 48
Urnfield culture 74–75
Uruk period 30, 32, 36

vassal states 37
    Assyrian empire 48, 53
    China 98
villages 104
    Bronze Age Europe 73
    Chayonu 23
    Eridu 28
    Fertile Crescent 22, 23, 26
    Natufians 22
Villanova culture 90
votive offerings *74*

Warring States period 99
warrior class 70, 72, 75, 79, 86, 98
weaponry 43, 61, *62*, 72, 73, 75, 79
weaving 19
wheat *see* cereals
wheel 19, 74
writing
    Chinese 98
    clay tablets 27, 57
    cuneiform 57
    hieroglyphic 79, 103, 104
    Greek 87
    Indus valley 94, 95
    Minoan 79
    Mycenaean 79, 87
    Olmec 103
    parchment 57
    Phoenician 87, 91
    pictographic 33, 94, 98
    syllabic script 79
    Ubaid culture 29
Wu, king of Zhou 99

Xerxes 57
Xia dynasty 98

Yellow River valley 98
Yu the Great 98

Zagros mountains 18, 23, 26
Zapotec civilization 10, 103–104
Zedekiah (king of Judah) 3
Zhou dynasty 96, 99
ziggurats 36